"Our capacity to make sense of early life experienc[] the ti[]me is a powerful source of healing. While we c[] form our lives from unresolved to resolved trauma through healing relationships, pani[]d by deep reflection on how the past has impacted us and what we can do, now, to cr[]ate new ways of feeling, thinking, and behaving. The powerful set of exercises in this []uided journal offers a way to make sense of your past and deepen how to identify and []hift adaptations to the challenging, adverse experiences you may have had in your life. []esearch suggests that this making-sense process is part of what can empower us to 'e[]rn' security in our attachment and free ourselves to live the life we've only dreamed migh[]t be possible."

——**Daniel J. Siegel, MD**, *New York Times* best-selling author of *Personality and Wholeness in Therapy, The Developing Mind, Mindsight, Parenting from the Inside Out*, and *Aware*

"Dor[]na Jackson Nakazawa expertly guides her reader toward a deep understanding of chil[]hood adversity and its lasting impact. With compassionate writing prompts, digestible []euroscience, and engaging mindfulness, her guided journal invites body and mind into []the healing process, creating an essential resource for individuals recovering from dev[]lopmental adversity."

——**Kelly McDaniel, LPC, NCC**, trauma therapist, and author of *Ready to Heal* and *Mother Hunger*

"Thi[] journal is a gem that will aid many in their journey to healing from childhood adversitie[]! Research consistently documents the benefits of expressing one's difficult experienc[]s in writing. But this workbook is much more than a guide to putting one's story on pap[]r. It shows how to weave healing compassion into the difficult memories of life—and reconnect mind, heart, and body through a very impressive array of skills. Very well don[]e!"

——**Glenn R. Schiraldi, PhD**, author of *The Adverse Childhood Experiences Recovery Workbook*; stress management faculties at the University of Maryland (ret.) and International Critical Incident Stress Foundation; founder of Resilience Training International

"Although the path to heal from childhood trauma is often confusing and challenging, Jackson Nakazawa is the gentle and clear guide needed for the journey. This journal offers survivors evidence-based, trauma-healing tools in accessible and straightforward ways, giving everyone who reads this access to agency, power, and healing. When more people have this tool—and can begin to heal from their childhood injuries—our communities, families, and future is more hopeful."

—**Hillary L. McBride, PhD**, registered psychologist, podcaster, speaker, and author of *The Wisdom of Your Body*

"*The Adverse Childhood Experiences Guided Journal* is packed with exercises that are carefully curated and expertly designed. Thoughtful, helpful, and gentle in its approach, this book will be a trusted resource for many adults who are healing from childhood trauma. It's destined to become a classic."

—**Hope Edelman**, grief and loss coach, author of *Motherless Daughters*, and founder and CEO at www.motherlessdaughters.com

"Donna Jackson Nakazawa offers a compassionate and humane approach to overcoming the wounds of adverse childhood experiences by encouraging us to transform our internal turmoil into insightful written reflections. Her gentle and kind spirit is palpable throughout the book, providing readers with a sense of comfort and support as they navigate their inner anguish. A must-read for anyone who is struggling with emotional challenges related to adverse early experiences!"

—**Ruth Lanius, MD, PhD**, professor of psychiatry, Harris-Woodman Chair, and director of the post-traumatic stress disorder (PTSD) research unit at the University of Western Ontario

The
Adverse
Childhood
Experiences
Guided Journal

Neuroscience-Based Writing Practices to Rewire Your Brain from Trauma

DONNA JACKSON NAKAZAWA

New Harbinger Publications, Inc.

Publisher's Note

This publication is designed to provide accurate and authoritative information in regard to the subject matter covered. It is sold with the understanding that the publisher is not engaged in rendering psychological, financial, legal, or other professional services. If expert assistance or counseling is needed, the services of a competent professional should be sought.

NEW HARBINGER PUBLICATIONS is a registered trademark of New Harbinger Publications, Inc.

New Harbinger Publications is an employee-owned company.

All Rights Reserved

Cover design by Amy Shoup

Interior design by Tom Comitta

Acquired by Tesilya Hanauer

Edited by Amber Williams

Printed in the United States of America

26   25   24

10   9   8   7   6   5   4   3   2   1   First Printing

Contents

🌿 Dedication

To you, whoever you are and however this finds you: you matter.
Your story matters. Here's to your story, your courage, and your healing.

Foreword

I was introduced to Donna Jackson Nakazawa's work by way of *Childhood Disrupted*, an influential book that unraveled the profound impacts of childhood trauma, shedding light on the enduring scars etched within us by our earliest experiences. Donna's research provided a compass to navigate the intricate terrain of childhood adversity, offering a beacon of understanding for those grappling with the aftermath of such formative years.

Childhood Disrupted acted as a catalyst, urging individuals to confront the shadows of their past and embark on a journey toward healing. Within these pages, Donna, a sage in understanding adverse childhood experiences (ACEs), unravels the complexities of childhood trauma and its lasting repercussions, which marked a turning point in the discourse surrounding mental health and well-being.

As I read *The Adverse Childhood Experiences Guided Journal*, I was struck by the tangible evolution of Donna's transformative work. This journal serves as a compass for those navigating the turbulent seas of their past, providing a structured and compassionate guide to the shores of healing. In these pages, Donna seamlessly combines practical activities with the profound knowledge honed over decades of dedication to trauma-sensitive care.

The power of this guided journal lies not just in its exercises but in the wealth of experience and empathy that Donna infuses into each page. It is a testament to her unwavering commitment to empowering individuals to confront their adverse childhood experiences and embark on self-discovery and healing.

Donna's journey into the heart of childhood adversity is not merely an academic pursuit but a profoundly personal and empathetic exploration. Her approach is one of both scientist and healer, seamlessly blending research-driven insights with a compassionate understanding of the human experience. Through her work, she illuminates the transformative potential that lies within each person's journey toward self-discovery and resilience.

As you embark on this guided journal, allow yourself the grace to navigate your narrative. Donna's voice gently accompanies you, offering support and insight as you delve into the recesses of your past. The activities within these pages are not just exercises—they are stepping stones toward reclaiming agency over your story and fostering a renewed sense of self.

The Adverse Childhood Experiences Guided Journal is not a collection of directives but an invitation to embark on a journey of introspection, self-compassion, and healing. Through each carefully crafted activity, Donna beckons you to explore the depths of your experiences and emerge with a newfound resilience.

In a world where the echoes of childhood adversity often reverberate through adulthood, this workbook stands as a beacon of hope. It is an invaluable resource for anyone seeking to understand, confront, and ultimately transcend the adversities that have shaped their lives.

May this guided journal be a trusted companion on your journey—one that empowers you to rewrite the narrative of your past and embrace a future filled with healing, resilience, and newfound strength.

With warmth and encouragement,
Nedra Glover Tawwab, LCSW

Welcome to the Adverse Childhood Experiences Guided Journal

Welcome! I'm so glad you're here.

This journal will help you recognize old, painful thought patterns; observe how your history of adversity may be affecting your health, relationships, work, and well-being; and begin rewriting your inner story.

In my thirty years as a science journalist, I've sat with and listened to thousands of individuals as they share their stories of adversity, self-discovery, and healing. Along the way, I've developed a series of neuroscience-based writing prompts and exercises to help individuals better reflect upon these deeply felt memories and gain new insights. These are simple but powerful questions to help you better understand how what happened to you in your childhood can still affect you now. I've taught this process to thousands of people at workshops, universities, and organizations around the country. These prompts, coupled with neuroscience-based mindfulness techniques, and other strategies, emerge from my many decades of reporting on the neuroscience of trauma and resilience in my award-winning books, *Girls on the Brink*, *The Angel and the Assassin*, *Childhood Disrupted*, *The Last Best Cure*, and *The Autoimmune Epidemic*. Every step in this process has been carefully curated to help you journey toward self-awareness, a new layer of emotional healing, and self-love. Healing is a journey. This book cannot take the place of professional help, but it can support your healing process.

Often people who take on demanding caregiving roles, or who are called to enter caring professions, have a history of greater adversity.

In interviewing hundreds of leading researchers and neuroscientists about adversity and resilience, one of the many things I've learned is this: Knowledge in and of itself is not enough to change old neural patterns. When we try to change our thought patterns and reactions on our own, we often automatically overlay old, ingrained thought patterns onto newly learned approaches.

Through the step-by-step guided writing exercises in this journal, a technique known as writing-to-heal, you will be able to translate your difficult childhood experiences into powerful written insights that help open the doorway to trauma recovery.

You'll learn how the *adverse childhood experiences* (ACEs) you've encountered have shaped your understanding of yourself. ACEs include the following: 1) growing up with a parent (or caregiver) who puts you down or makes fun of you, 2) growing up in a family that doesn't really seem to care about your well-being, 3) having parents who separate or divorce, or losing a parent, 4) growing up with a parent who suffers from a mental health condition or substance use disorder, and 5) experiencing physical or sexual abuse. Additional ACEs include growing up with violence in your home; being bullied by peers or siblings; being separated from parents through foster care or adoption; and facing systemic racism, discrimination, and poverty.

Why is it so important to examine how these early experiences might be affecting your well-being? When you experience adverse childhood experiences, you need the adults around you to keep you safe, reassure you that you are loved, and assure you that you are not to blame for what's happening. When the adults in your life don't do these things (perhaps they lack the skills or are struggling with their own issues), you begin to believe that what's happening to you must be your fault. This can trigger the belief that there is something wrong with *you*. This belief takes hold early on—when you are too young to question it—and can stay with you throughout your life, shaping your view of who you are. These messages you've internalized have not yet been examined and rewritten.

This ACEs Guided Journal has been carefully crafted to help you make that essential leap to understand that there is nothing wrong with you. There is nothing wrong with who you are. It is designed to help you not only rewrite those beliefs and messages that took hold inside you when you were young but also to create a new internal—and very personalized—playbook for lifelong flourishing.

You'll also learn an array of science-based mindfulness approaches which, coupled with curated writing prompts, will help you to uncover internal resources for resiliency. This two-pronged approach, which I call *neural re-narrating*, will help you to create new, more powerful, resonant, and purposeful healing narratives that will help you to flourish in your life. This is a powerful process because it helps you override your brain's old, habitual reactions and create new, healthier responses that change your brain and nervous system.

My hope is that you'll come away with simple but powerful tools and a new healing narrative that you can carry with you wherever you go, one that enhances and helps you to create a deeper sense of resiliency and we1ll-being.

By doing this work, you will not only help yourself through difficulties from the past as well as in your present life but you will also begin to extend that sense of safety to help others you care about to thrive too.

Medical Disclaimer: The exercises you are about to participate in contain material that may cause some individuals (especially those with a history of trauma, developmental trauma, PTSD, or mental health concerns, including anxiety or depression) to have strong reactions, feelings, or memories. For this reason, discretion is advised. The contents, writing prompts, and information in this journal are not to be perceived as or relied upon in any way as medical advice or mental health advice. Nor are they a substitute for professional or medical advice, diagnosis, or treatment. A guided journal can help you to better understand your story and to address your childhood wounds, but it is not a substitute for therapy or professional support.

Please seek the advice of mental health professionals or other qualified health providers with any questions you may have regarding whether this guided journal is right for you.

The goal of this journal is to help you:

- Recognize the effect that adverse childhood experiences may have on your view of yourself and on your adult health and well-being.

- Create new habits of self-talk and a series of life-enhancing, self-compassionate practices that help you to create joy within yourself and transform your life.

- Feel more wholeheartedly present and there for yourself and others.

- Recognize the deep well of resources you hold within yourself—and which brought you here today.

- Safely bring forth a deep sense of comfort and gladness for exactly who you are right now, and for who you have always been.

- View yourself with affection, self-respect, and a sense of loyalty to yourself.

- Move away from harsh self-criticism, judgment, and anger toward yourself or others.

- Find a new sense of inner peace when there is chaos around you.

- Enhance your emotional and physical well-being through a sense of centered calm that is not shaken by the behavior or actions of others.

- Know you are well on your way to having the resources to cope with life's inevitable challenges and hardships now and in the future.

🌿 Your Biology Is Not Your Destiny

In the early parts of this journal, you will learn some of the science on how facing chronic stressors and trauma in childhood can affect the brain and immune system in ways that influence your physical and mental health. It's important to remember that the adversity you've faced does not define you. Your biology is not your destiny. Neuroscience tells us that the wonderfully neuroplastic brain is exquisitely responsive to intervention once we figure out how to intervene.

By working to overcome the impact of trauma, you can begin to create healthier neural connections in the brain. It's a bit like doing physical therapy for your mind!

⚜ How to Get the Most Out of This Journal

I recommend you find a quiet space. You want to choose somewhere where it feels safe and private. Wear comfy clothes. You'll want to have pencils, pens, colored pencils, a black marker, writing paper, notecards, or Post-its available.

I encourage you to make this journal your own! It can be as simple or as artistic as you would like to make it. Feel free to add your own touches (e.g., tie your journal together with ribbon; add more photos, drawings, or notes). Ultimately, you are creating a book that you can revisit anytime as you continue on your healing journey.

Finally, I recommend you gather photos of significant people who have loved or mentored you, or with whom you feel safe and loved. These can include a loving adult, friend, pet, or even a spiritual figure. It will also be helpful to gather photos of yourself as a child, teenager, and young adult. I suggest you put these photos in an envelope and tuck the envelope into the back of your journal. You'll want to have them on hand when you begin part 4, Finding Your Benefactors, and again in part 6, Learning the Power of Kind Self-Talk.

A few words about how this book is structured: The first few parts of this book include many different writing exercises, as well as short informative sections about how and why trauma and adverse childhood experiences can affect your lifelong emotional and physical health. Learning this information will give you a strong foundation to keep doing the deeper writing-to-heal work and aid in your healing journey as you work through this journal. The second part of this journal will take you even deeper into the process of writing-to-heal, helping you to reimagine and rewrite your inner story, opening the door to new layers of well-being.

Caring for Yourself through the Journey

I want to be sure that you're prepared with ways to take care of yourself as you begin your healing journey. Feel free to come back to this self-care lesson at any point. You are in charge of your healing journey, so do what feels most comfortable to you. Please work through this journal at whatever pace feels good to you. You may even want to consider undertaking this work while partnering with a friend or while working with a therapist.

In this journal, you'll be reflecting on different feelings and memories that can be painful. If at any point anything feels too overwhelming or too difficult, please stop and take care of yourself. It is *okay* to take a break whenever you need to. Go for a walk. Do some deep breathing. Call a friend. Reach out to a trusted mental health care practitioner.

As you work through this journal, you'll learn many new ways to take care of yourself and calm your physical and mental state when you feel overwhelmed. Please use the tools as often as possible now that you are dedicating yourself to learning them.

I invite you to participate in each activity as fully as you can and to allow yourself, if it feels right to you, to move through any initial resistance you might feel. This interior sense of resistance might sound like, "I don't have time to do this!" or "This is silly!" or "Writing about my feelings can't help me."

Often these self-doubts arise from feeling unworthy of self-care, or from feeling that taking care of others is more important than making efforts on your own behalf, or even from a sense of uncertainty as to what might unfold.

Bring a heartfelt sense of self-compassion and affection for yourself, as well as the courage, fortitude, and desire to flourish that brought you here, to do this work. It's not important how many words you write, or whether you do an exercise in a certain way, or in a certain time frame. There is no right way.

Give yourself permission to let go of all self-judgment and simply allow yourself to gift these moments of your life to yourself. Finally, please commit to setting aside a few moments each day to dive safely within and to participate in each activity.

🌿 The Power of Your Breath

As part of your self-care as you dive into your own story, please be sure to take time to notice how you are breathing. Why does this matter? Your nervous system is comprised of an intricate network that carries messages from the brain to the body—telling you whether you are safe or not safe—in order to help you regulate your bodily functions and prepare for any possible challenges in your environment. This network is a two-way superhighway of messaging.

Messages from the body tell the brain whether you're safe, and the brain sends messages to the body about whether you need to prepare for any potential threat. One of the ways in which the body and brain communicate is through the breath. You take in 25,000 breaths a day.

If your breath is shallow or coming quickly, as it is when you are stressed, the brain gets the message to act and respond as if you're in physical danger.

Your emotional state of mind affects the rate, depth, and pattern of your breath and vice versa.

How Does Breathing Help?

According to decades of research, the most beneficial breath sequence for stimulating the positive healing power of the nervous system, calming your brain and body, and managing anxiety is breathing in for 5 1/2 seconds and breathing out for 5 1/2 seconds (Lin, Tai, and Fan 2014).

Filling your diaphragm—by pushing your belly out like a Buddha belly—also helps push blood into the heart and slow your heart rate. Slowing your heart rate helps to pump blood throughout the body, thus oxygenating the body and brain. This helps stimulate the relaxation response.

Although many medicines can temporarily dampen the stress response, there are no medications you can take to boost the relaxation response. Slow, gentle breathing can stimulate the relaxation response rapidly and effectively—in as little as five minutes.

The oldest tool we have is the most powerful—the breath—and it has zero side effects.

🌿 Self-Care Activity: Five-Point Breathing with Three Mindful Sighs

One technique you can use to calm your brain, body, and nervous system is to take five-point breaths and then let them go as long, mindful sighs. When you're ready, give it a try.

Instructions

Let's try five-point breaths. As we take in these breaths, we're going to extend it to five points of the body, which calms the nervous system. Inhale slowly, and as you do, take in a deep five-point breath, consciously breathing into:

- Your nostrils

- The back of your throat

- Your upper chest

- Your belly—feeling your belly fill as completely as you can, letting it expand

- Now feel the breath rise up your spine from your tailbone up to the top of your head and feel this column fill with light and breath

Now as you exhale, let out a long, audible sigh—just let everything go.

Inhale slowly again, focusing on all five points, letting the breath out with another big, audible sigh. *Ahhhhh.* And again. *Ahhhhh.* How do you feel?

When we practice slower five-point breathing, as we just did, we increase blood flow to the brain in areas that help us gain emotional clarity and insight into our own story.

This increased blood flow also helps us to feel safe and centered, so that we can commit to caring for our own needs. As we exhale and let the breath go in a slow, mindful sigh, we quiet the nervous system.

For some individuals with a history of trauma or abuse, focusing on the breath can activate triggers that are, instead of calming, a source of discomfort or dysregulation. If this is the case with any of the breath-awareness exercises in this journal, please stop and seek professional therapeutic help to further explore your inner experience.

🌿 Warming Up Your Writing Muscles

Below is a simple warm-up exercise that has helped me when I engage in expressive writing. You may already be writing or journaling regularly. Or you may be a beginner to expressive writing. Either is totally fine. You don't need to have any special writing skills to reap the benefits of this writing-to-heal program. I hope the following exercise will help you to feel more comfortable and at ease as you begin to put your pen or pencil to paper.

Exercise

Put your pencil to your paper and just start to go around in circles on the paper for a minute.

Feel any uncertainty. Notice what you feel in your body, your emotions, not knowing what will be revealed.

What is it that brought you here?

What do you hope to gain by being here?

Now, simply draw circles again. The point here is to break any resistance you might feel to putting words on the page.

On some level, we are all here for similar reasons. Now put pen and paper down, close your eyes if you'd like, and go within and see what emerges for you as you sit in stillness. Notice any bodily sensations.

Check in to see if you are holding any tightness or tension in your jaws, shoulders, chest, belly, pelvis, thighs, or feet. See if you can gently invite that tightness to let go.

🌿 Open the Door to the Self-Space

On brain scans (Tian et al. 2021), individuals who've experienced adversity in childhood often show changes in connectivity in what's known as the *default mode network*, or DMN, an area of the brain that we might also think of as the *self-space*.

The DMN is associated with self-related thoughts—your sense of who you are, the narrative that you create about yourself for good or for ill—which, in turn, affects your ability to care for yourself, practice self-compassion, and find resiliency throughout your life.

Disrupted neural connectivity in this self-space can make it difficult to process and make sense of your own story.

Often, people who take on demanding caregiving roles, or who are called to enter caring professions, have a history of great adversity. They may unconsciously devote themselves to caregiving roles as a way of trying to make meaning out of and resolve their own trauma.

Often, this is because those who've experienced trauma want to help others feel seen, known, and valued, and offer up avenues of healing, as they themselves would like to have been helped, seen, and known when they suffered in their own childhood. Indeed, studies on "wounded healers" show us that those with a history of childhood adversity are more likely to become therapists, social workers, and nurses (Brown et al. 2022; Clark and Aboueissa 2021).

And yet, those with a history of adversity and trauma often struggle the most with their own self-care. Individuals who have a history of trauma are also more likely to feel a sense of resistance within when they try to engage in self-compassionate practices, making staying with self-care practices more difficult. Providing high levels of caregiving to others, coupled with low levels of self-care and self-compassion, is a trauma state of mind and it's hard to dislodge.

Writing-to-heal can help you to promote healthier neural connectivity in the default mode network, which is associated with an enhanced ability to process self-related thoughts and increased mindful awareness.

Tending to your own emotional well-being with self-compassion matters in whether you're able to stay calm, centered, and well-regulated when you are under stress, or when others around you are struggling and are not well-regulated. Self-compassion helps you to be emotionally and physically centered and healthy enough to help others, whether it's your children, students, clients, patients, family members, colleagues, or friends.

Neural re-narrating through writing-to-heal combined with mindfulness-based practices is a powerful way to open the door to that self-space, and to do so with a sense of compassion for yourself. Before you get started on the next lesson, I'd like you to practice a simple self-care tool that can have a powerful calming and healing effect on body and mind.

Self-Care Activity: Activate a Soothing Inner Vibration

Another powerful practice that helps you care for yourself when you feel overwhelmed and helps dampen the stress response and stimulate relaxation is the practice of letting out the simple sound of OMMM slowly and repeatedly. Research shows that the experience of vibration of sound around the ears and throughout the body is transmitted to the vagus nerve.

The vagus nerve is the largest nerve in the body. It sends trillions of messages from your limbic system in your brain—where your primal fear response is lodged—down to all the organs of your body, regulating your heart rate, respiration in your lungs, your digestion, and so on.

Instructions:

To begin, gently close your eyes.

Place one hand over your collarbone and your other hand over your heart. Take in a long inhale—5 1/2 seconds in—and slowly let out a longer exhale, making the exhale longer than the inhale, while letting out the sound OMMMMM.

Let's do this again. As you do it, you should feel a gentle, warm vibration under your hands.

Feel this soothing inner sound as it vibrates and fills your body.

Let's take in another breath and then let out the sound, OMMMM. See how long you can make your exhale last. You might imagine yourself singing out this sound.

Feel this soothing, gentle vibration spread through your chest, belly, face, and head, and imagine it extending into your arms, legs, hands, and feet.

You might even imagine the sound carries with it a white, healing, protective light that travels and spreads throughout your body into every cell.

And again, let's take in a breath and let out the sound of OMMM and let it last as long as you comfortably can. OMMMMM.

This practice can help to cultivate what's known as vagal tone. Improving vagal tone helps to promote a sense of interior resiliency, safety, and calm.

How did that self-care activity feel?

_____

_____

_____

_____

_____

Notice anything that may feel different. Do you feel a little bit calmer?

_____

_____

_____

_____

_____

If so, can you name that feeling (it might be something simple like "relaxed" or "less anxious")?

_____

_____

_____

_____

_____

Do you feel any sense of relaxation in your body? If so, can you name where that feeling is in your body—in your chest, face, or jaw?

_____

_____

_____

_____

_____

Part 1: Looking Back at Your Story

Time stops inside their wounds, seemingly never to heal.
—Hope Jahren

In order to understand how your past history of adversity can influence your emotional well-being in the present, we need to go back in time. Here, we're going to look back at your story to get an overview of experiences you had in childhood. This includes experiences that might have been challenging or traumatic, as well as positive experiences and influences that helped you during difficult times in your childhood. You'll also look at your sense of well-being in your current daily life and you'll set an intention for what you want to get out of this journal as you engage in your personal journey toward flourishing.

As you get ready to examine your story, what words come to mind? These might be words like "curious" or "complicated" or "stressful." There are no right words. Just choose the first few words that come up.

_____

_____

_____

_____

Now, if you were to give your own story a movie or book title, what would that be? Get creative. But don't overthink it! It might be something like "My Teenage Years of Loss and Loneliness" or "The Girl Whose Mother Didn't Like Her" or "The Boy Who Had No Adults to Lean On" or "The Secrets I Learned to Keep" or "How My Family Wounded Me." Make this your own!

_____

_____

_____

Trauma and the Brain

Adversity in childhood can change the brain in myriad ways, altering neural connectivity in the *amygdala*, the alarm center of the brain; the *hippocampus*, where you process memories and emotions; the *pre-frontal cortex*, the decision-making center of your brain; and other important areas. Changes also occur in neural integration between key brain areas, affecting how well these areas communicate with each other (Teicher and Samson 2016). These changes can profoundly affect how you feel on a day-to-day basis, including how well you're able to:

- Recognize your own feelings and fears.

- Accurately perceive and interpret events happening around you.

- Voice what you need and want especially when under stress.

- Focus on what you need or require to feel safe, calm, and centered in challenging moments.

- Use your ability to calm yourself and self-regulate when you encounter challenges in your life—for instance, an argument with your spouse, teenager, or colleague.

You may sometimes find yourself either overreacting or underreacting to the world around you more than you'd like, feel powerless about how you can exert influence over your history of adversity, or experience a sense of inertia or hopelessness about how you can manage chronic stressors now.

Do you feel you sometimes have big, overwhelming reactions? Perhaps you become angry, anxious, or feel hurt in a way that feels out of proportion to what's happening or say things you don't mean. If so, please don't judge yourself! This is very common and you are already in the process of changing your habitual reactions by completing this journal.

If you feel you do sometimes have big overreactions, what do they look like?

Do you feel that you sometimes underreact to difficult situations? Perhaps you shut down, or instead of speaking up for yourself, you ruminate about what happened versus taking action. If so, don't judge yourself! This, too, is very common. If you feel you underreact, what does this look like?

If you have a history of adverse childhood experiences, you may find that you spend a lot of time, energy, and headspace trying to manage your own feelings. When you're flooded with emotions, it can be harder to focus on the situation in front of you and see those around you—children, family, colleagues, clients, or patients—for who they are and what they may need for their healing and thriving.

Ask yourself to commit to engaging in this heartfelt effort to wake up on your own side, to find new layers of healing and flourishing in your life.

It's hard to soothe others when you're caught up in trying to soothe yourself. When you're caught up in managing your own emotions and anxieties, children you love or care about can't feel seen, known, soothed, and secure. Adults who've found internal resources to flourish, even in adversity, are better able to thrive and help others feel safe and regulated.

Take a moment to reflect here on people in your life for whom you'd like to be more present, calm, and centered. In addition to yourself (you come first!), who would benefit from you becoming more self-regulated in the face of life's inevitable difficulties and challenges? These often include our children, partners, or coworkers.

Who would you like to show up for in a calmer and more self-regulated way?

You can begin to change the legacy of the past by learning and applying neuroscience-based techniques that have a calming and regulating effect that is compassionate, patient, kind, and accepting of yourself.

The intention is to become the "general contractor" of your own well-being and engage in the neuroscience-based prompts and tools in this journal to replace old neural pathways that no longer serve you with neural pathways that promote your healing and flourishing. This is the process that I call neural re-narrating.

Adverse Childhood Experiences (ACEs)

I'd like to take a moment here to explain a bit more about what adverse childhood experiences (ACEs) are and why learning about them is so important to your health.

The term adverse childhood experiences refers to chronic, unpredictable stressors that children and teenagers encounter while growing up. The ACEs questionnaire was first created in 1995 by a team of physicians who asked thousands of patients about their experiences in childhood and then compared those childhood experiences to the patients' adult health records.

This original ACEs survey asks about ten categories of adversity in childhood. These include facing physical, emotional, or sexual abuse; physical or emotional neglect; and experiencing different types of familial dysfunction, including growing up with a parent who suffered from a mental illness or addiction, parents who separated or divorced, or a parent who left.

Adverse childhood experiences turn out to have a profound effect on adult health. Over two thousand studies have shown that individuals with ACE scores of 2 or more are more likely to develop physical and mental health concerns in adulthood. This relationship between adversity in childhood and health issues in adulthood is dose-dependent. In other words, the more categories of ACEs you experienced as a child, the greater the likelihood of later experiencing physical and mental health disorders in adulthood.

For instance, women with an ACE score of 3 have a 60 percent increased risk of later developing an autoimmune disease, such as lupus, multiple sclerosis, or Type 1 diabetes (Dube et al. 2009). And those with an ACEs score of 4 or more are 4 times more likely to experience depression in adulthood (Desch et al. 2023). Please remember that the ACEs survey did not study the role of interventions and strategies to help ameliorate the ill effects of adversity. Therefore, these findings are not etched in stone. The brain remains neuroplastic—and able to change—throughout life.

Now, if any of this feels overwhelming, please remember to go at your own pace. Know that as we work together to understand this link between the past and the present, you will begin to make new meaning out of your narrative and your story in ways that will help you to flourish in your everyday life.

Your safety matters more than anything else. In the questionnaires that follow, you will be asked about your childhood. For individuals who have experienced significant developmental trauma, including early, intense, chronic abuse or neglect, feelings may emerge which require more effective therapy and support than that which a guided journal can provide. These may emerge as feelings of shame or that one is wrong or defective; the inability to regulate one's emotions or calm oneself down; hopelessness or helplessness; dissociation; or even harm directed at the individual themself. For more on how to find therapeutic help, please see the resources section at the end of this book. If you or anyone you know is in crisis, please contact the National Suicide Prevention Lifeline at 988.

Questionnaires

First, you'll take a questionnaire that examines the adversity you may have faced in childhood. Then, you'll take a questionnaire that measures your positive childhood experiences, followed by one that examines the joy you find in everyday life.

I want to be clear here that we are not using these questionnaires and checklists as a form of screening for types of childhood adversity you might have faced. Instead, I'd like you to see these as a means of helping you to lean in and listen to the narrative of your own story, the challenges you've faced in your life, and the ways in which you've found resiliency, even in the face of adversity.

These three questionnaires are simply a way of helping you to get a better snapshot of where you are in your healing process at this point in time. I have found in my own life that using these surveys as a simple tool to listen within has helped me to gain powerful insight into both my past and my present life. This understanding has clarified my hopes and aspirations on my journey toward flourishing.

These questions may shed new light on your experiences growing up or on the extent of the adversity you faced. It is normal to feel uncertain or even overwhelmed the first time you answer questions about your adverse childhood experiences. Or you may experience a sense of relief at seeing the link between past events and your current life for the first time. All of these reactions are perfectly normal. Often, the healing path toward resiliency and thriving begins with recognizing the role that ACEs play in adult well-being and suffering.

Original Ten Categories of ACEs Questionnaire

Instructions: Below is a list of the original ten categories of adverse childhood experiences (ACEs). From the list below, please place a checkmark next to each ACE category that you experienced prior to your eighteenth birthday. Then, please add up the number of categories of ACEs you experienced and put the total number at the bottom.

1. **Physical Neglect.** Did you feel that you didn't have enough to eat, had to wear dirty clothes, and had no one to protect you? Or that your parents didn't take you to the doctor if you needed it?

2. **Loss of a Parent.** Did you lose a parent through separation, divorce, abandonment, death, or other reason?

3. **Parent with Mental Illness.** Did you live with anyone who was depressed, mentally ill, or attempted suicide?

4. **Parent with Addiction in Home.** Did you live with anyone who had a problem with drinking or using drugs, including prescription drugs?

5. **Witnessing Parents Be Abused.** Did your parents or adults in your home ever hit, punch, beat, or threaten to harm each other?

6. **Incarcerated Family Member.** Did you live with anyone who went to jail or prison?

7. **Emotional Abuse.** Did a parent or adult in your home ever swear at you, insult you, humiliate you, or put you down?

8. **Physical Abuse.** Did a parent or adult in your home ever hit, beat, grab, slap, kick, or physically hurt you in any way?

9. **Emotional Neglect.** Did you feel that no one in your family loved you or thought you were important or special? Or did you feel your family didn't look out for each other, feel close to each other, or support each other?

10. **Sexual Abuse.** Did you experience unwanted sexual contact (such as fondling or being touched in a sexual way)?

(For more on the original ten categories of ACEs, see the references listed at the end of this book.)

Let's take a moment to notice and reflect on what stood out for you as you completed the ACEs questionnaire above. **Did you find that you faced more than one type of adverse childhood experience?** If so, you are not alone. This is very common.

_____

_____

_____

_____

_____

_____

Which of these categories of adversity feel especially emotionally charged for you as you answered this questionnaire? For example, if you experienced three categories of ACEs, it may be that one or two stood out as having had a more potent effect on how you see yourself now or the narrative that you've created about your life.

_____

_____

_____

_____

_____

_____

_____

Simply write a few words to note what stood out to you. It might be, "Nobody ever had my back" or "Always feeling criticized." If all of the adversities you faced were equally challenging, that is perfectly normal too. **Just jot down a few words now to make a note of what resonated the most while you were filling out this questionnaire.**

_____

_____

_____

_____

How did noticing and writing down your responses above feel? What emotions did it bring up? This might be sadness or worry (perhaps over how these past traumas might still affect you today). Many people report feeling a sense of loss, worry, or overwhelm when first completing this questionnaire.

Please fill in the blanks in the sentence below:

When I think about how _____

_____

(e.g., "Nobody had my back" or "My mother always put me down" or "My parents hated each other"),

I feel _____

_____

(these might include feelings like angry, sad, overwhelmed, tearful, afraid, resentful).

Expanded ACEs Checklist

Researchers now recognize there are many other categories that qualify as ACEs. The second ACEs checklist looks at additional types of adversity in childhood that can have an effect on your long-term mental and physical health:

- Growing up in poverty or with excessive financial worries

- Growing up in a violent neighborhood

- Losing a close family member or friend to death

- Facing chronic bullying by a sibling or at school/by peers

- Facing medical trauma as a child

- Growing up with a parent, caregiver, or sibling who faced serious or chronic medical issues/chronic illness

- Being separated from your parent or caregiver for weeks or months, including adoption, or being in foster care

- Facing racism or discrimination

- Growing up with poor housing quality or attending substandard schools

- Facing an environmental crisis or disaster such as earthquakes, wildfires, or a pandemic

As you consider the expanded ACEs checklist, what category felt most emotionally charged for you?

What feelings came up for you? Please fill in the blanks when you think about the adversity you faced.

When I think about _____

_____,

I feel _____

_____.

Write a few more words about how facing this adversity still affects how you see yourself now or the narrative that you've created about your life. It might be, for instance, "I was always worried my dad would die and now I'm always worried I'll lose someone." Or it might be, "I was bullied a lot at school, and I still find it hard to trust people I meet."

_____

_____

_____

_____

_____

_____

Questions to Ponder

In addition to the questions you answered on the ten categories of ACEs questionnaire and the expanded ACEs checklist, think about the impact other painful events might have had on you. As you read through the questions below, write down any emotions that arise. This might be "Yes, this terrified me when it happened" or "Yes, I could never please my dad," and so on.)

Did your parents or caregivers:

- **Live or stay together in an atmosphere of tension, resentment, arguing, or bitterness over extended periods of time?**

_____

_____

_____

_____

- **Threaten to divorce each other?**

_____

_____

_____

_____

- Require perfection or extremely high achievement, expect you to "measure up" (and if you fell short, express major disappointment or put you down)?

_____

_____

_____

_____

- Punish you with silence or isolation?

_____

_____

_____

_____

- Focus on your weight or appearance or diet?

_____

_____

_____

_____

- Keep you from exploring the world, even when it was safe and appropriate?

_____

_____

_____

_____

- Rely on your accomplishments for their sense of self-worth?

_____

_____

_____

- Respond to you by behaving in confusingly erratic ways so that you had to spend a lot of mental energy figuring out how to please them?

- Have an explosive temper?

- Rely on manipulation or coercion so that you were compliant with their wishes?

_____

_____

_____

_____

_____

🌿 Positive Childhood Experiences

Now that you understand the adversities you faced in childhood, let's look at the positive experiences and influences that might have helped you—even during times of difficulty in childhood or during your teenage years. In this next questionnaire, you'll explore sources of support that have helped you to find resiliency, even in the face of life's challenges, and focus on the things in your life that have supported you.

Bear in mind that having a high number of categories of ACEs in and of itself is a sign of your innate resiliency. This is true even if your positive childhood experience (PCE) score is low. A high number of ACEs underscores how remarkable you had to be as a child to survive a difficult childhood, as well as how adaptive you have had to be as an adult to deal with the aftermath of childhood trauma. Both of these require extraordinary resiliency.

Learning Your Positive Childhood Experiences Score:

From the list below, please place a checkmark next to each category of positive childhood experiences that applied to you <u>often/very often</u> before the age of eighteen and put the total number at the bottom.

Did you feel <u>often/very often</u>:

1. You were able to talk to your family about feelings.

2. Your family stood by you at difficult times.

3. You enjoyed participating in community traditions.

4. You felt a sense of belonging in high school.

5. You felt supported by friends.

6. You had at least two non-parent adults who took a genuine interest in you.

7. You felt safe and protected by an adult in your home.

Researchers have found that these positive childhood experiences are protective against adversity (Bethell et al. 2019). For instance, for those who experienced just 3 to 5 PCEs, their rate of depression was 50 percent lower than for those who had just 0 to 2 PCEs.

In considering your positive childhood experiences, which resonated for you the most?

Write about a memory of a particular person or mentor who helped you to feel seen, valued, and worthy—like a relative, neighbor, or teacher.

_____

_____

_____

_____

_____

Many individuals who experienced childhood adversity also report how they had to rely on their inner resourcefulness to help them through difficult experiences. Use the following thought prompts to explore this.

When you were struggling or worried, were you often able to find someone you trusted to confide in?

_____

_____

_____

_____

_____

When you look back at your childhood, did people around you notice that you were capable or independent for your age?

Were you determined to do well academically or in other areas of your life despite the adversity you faced?

What about your own capability and fortitude stands out the most?

_____

_____

_____

_____

_____

What emotions come up for you when you consider your own fortitude as a child?

_____

_____

_____

_____

_____

Joy and Contentment Quotient Inventory (JCQ-Inventory)

Now that you have explored the adversity and trauma you may have faced in childhood, as well as the positive experiences that helped you find resiliency during those years, we are going to move into the present and explore your sense of satisfaction and well-being in your daily life. The Joy and Contentment Quotient Inventory was originally designed by Marla Sanzone, PhD (Jackson Nakazawa 2013), and helps you focus on where you are now in terms of the degree of calm, peace, and joy that you're able to feel in your life and how able you are to be present and feel a deep sense of contentment in your current lived experience.

Circle 1-10, according to the degree to which each statement applies to you or accurately describes your recent (past three months) perception(s).

1 = does not apply to me much at all / hardly describes my perception at all

10 = nearly completely describes my perception / applies to me

1. **I feel deserving of a calm mind and a joyful life.**

   1   2   3   4   5   6   7   8   9   10

2. **I am more self-critical and judgmental than I wish I were.**

   1   2   3   4   5   6   7   8   9   10

3. **I recognize and value the unique contributions I bring to the world.**

   1   2   3   4   5   6   7   8   9   10

4. In general, my negative feelings and thoughts impact my ability to fully engage with my life, including but not limited to people and situations or events.

   1   2   3   4   5   6   7   8   9   10

5. I am more critical and judgmental of others than I wish I were.

   1   2   3   4   5   6   7   8   9   10

6. I am touched or moved emotionally by things in my environment every day that remind me of the goodness around me.

   1   2   3   4   5   6   7   8   9   10

7. Generally speaking, my feelings or emotional states overwhelm me.

   1   2   3   4   5   6   7   8   9   10

8. At least once a week, I allow myself to be spontaneous and playful without feeling guilty, despite my daily obligations and responsibilities.

   1   2   3   4   5   6   7   8   9   10

9. My feelings provide me information, but they do not control me nor my decisions.

   1   2   3   4   5   6   7   8   9   10

10. In going about my daily routine, I have difficulty being productive or completing necessary tasks without detaching from or shutting off my emotions.

1   2   3   4   5   6   7   8   9   10

11. I know specific things I want or need to change in my life, but I have a hard time putting forth sufficient effort to effectively implement them.

1   2   3   4   5   6   7   8   9   10

12. I am open to new and different interpretations of my experiences.

1   2   3   4   5   6   7   8   9   10

Scoring:

For questions 1, 3, 6, 8, 9, and 12: add up the exact numerical value of each answer you circled. For instance, if you circled a "4" for question 1 and a "7" for 3, add 4 and 7 and continue to add the number value of each answer for these questions.

Put your score here: _____

For questions 2, 4, 5, 7, 10, and 11: add up your scores in the reverse direction. In other words, a "1" gets 10 points whereas a "10" gets 1 point. A "2" would get 9 points. A "4" would be 7 points and so on. This chart can help:

Put your score here: _____

1=10	6=5
2=9	7=4
3=8	8=3
4=7	9=2
5=6	10=1

Now, add up your two scores: _____

Less than 38 total points: Significantly less contentment and considerably fewer moments of joy than most report experiencing. Could benefit from concerted effort toward increasing both for greater life satisfaction and feelings of well-being.

39-59 points: Occasional but not frequent sense of general contentment and few moments of joy that you are likely not inclined to expect. Average or "middle of the road" sense of life satisfaction and well-being. You may desire more experiences of joy and an increased sense of happiness, but may recognize a tendency toward pessimism and a general belief that you don't deserve or shouldn't expect more positive experiences than you have.

56-78 points: General sense of contentment and occasional moments of joy that you look forward to and work toward. Above average sense of life satisfaction and overall positive view of self and the world around you. You believe you deserve a satisfying life, generally are not overly pessimistic, and at times have a relatively optimistic but not idealistic worldview.

Above 79 points: Considerably higher sense of contentment and fairly frequent experiences of joy. Greater general life satisfaction and well-being than most. You tend toward optimism and at times even idealism, which you are likely to find refreshing and fun.

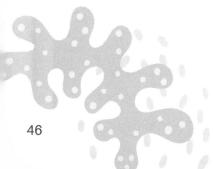

What questions—and answers—stood out to you above? If it's an awareness of being judgmental of yourself or that you don't notice the goodness in the world around you as much as you'd like—simply make a note of what felt most true for you.

_____

_____

_____

_____

What would you like to experience more or less of in your moment-to-moment life? If it's the ability to have more fun or be more spontaneous, or to feel more deserving of good things in your life, simply make a note of that here.

_____

_____

_____

_____

 Setting an Intention

Now that you've gained more insight into your own story, let's set a deeper intention about what you hope to gain from the journey you'll be taking throughout the rest of this journal.

To begin, gently close your eyes. Take in a deep breath, and let it go. As you breathe in again, focus your attention on your breath coming in through your nostrils, into your chest, and let it expand through your belly. And let it go. Take in another breath. Feel it expand throughout your body. And let it go.

Now, respond to the following questions:

What is it that brought you here?

_____

_____

_____

_____

What do you hope to get out of this journal?

_____

_____

_____

_____

Recognize and allow yourself to feel any uncertainty that arises. Notice what you feel in your body and your emotions as you embark on this new healing journey. You can ask yourself to commit to engaging in this heartfelt effort to be your greatest advocate and to find new layers of healing and flourishing in your life.

Perhaps you're hoping to learn to be less critical and judgmental of yourself. Or to retrain your anxious brain. Or to feel calmer and less reactive to others even when there is chaos and uncertainty swirling all around you.

Or perhaps you want to feel that the trauma you've experienced has less of a hold on you so you feel a greater sense of joy, relief, and safety in your life now and less anxiety or fear.

Whatever it is you hope to gain by being here, set that intention for yourself now.

Setting a positive intention helps to calm and soothe the nervous system. It also helps you to feel safe even with uncertainty, which helps pave the way for greater change.

Again, what is your intention? What do you hope to gain by being here? Take a few minutes to write about your intentions below.

Self-Care Activity: Soothe Your Inner Child

If you were not well-nurtured in childhood, you may feel some resistance when turning caring attention toward yourself. It may even feel silly to focus on your inner child. It is okay if doing the following exercise feels hard right now. Over time, however, this can be one of the most important self-soothing skills we can learn.

Instructions

Imagine that you are holding yourself as an infant and you are the mother or father to the child you once were. If you have already found and set aside a picture of your younger self, take that out now and gaze at the photo. Imagine wanting the best for that child and seeing the miracle of her or him. Hold her, coo or sing to her, lean down to kiss her forehead. In your mind's eye, rock her in your arms.

You might smooth your hand over your long-ago infant self's head, noticing the texture of her hair. Feel the weight of her as you hold her. Notice any small details about yourself as an infant. What color are your eyes? What is the shape of your nose? Your lips?

Imagine holding your infant self's tiny hand in yours or feeling her fingers wrap around your finger.

We call this long-ago child self your inner child.

Now, imagine your inner child feeling totally safe, loved, and cared for. You might imagine her letting out a long, audible sigh, the way that children do when they feel completely safe and loved in a caregiver's arms in that small moment, just before they drift off to sleep.

Imagine that you are the parent who sees and recognizes the beauty of who you are.

You might tell her you will always love her, care for her, and keep her safe as you continue on this healing journey and learn new approaches to better caring for yourself.

🌿 Draw Your Inner Child

Draw an image to reflect the infant you once were, held by yourself as the loving adult who parents, sees, knows, and recognizes the beauty of that child. It can be any image at all—abstract, a symbol, or figure.

Part 2: Finding Safety

There is no agony like bearing an untold story inside you.
—Zora Neale Hurston

It is said that suffering is not having anyone to tell your story to. The simple act of writing about an emotion, such as fear, anger, frustration, or shame, influences your physical and emotional state. Research shows that writing about such events helps to bring trauma out of the body by getting it on the page (Glass et al. 2019; Pennebaker et al. 1988).

If you're responding to the world with old feelings due to unresolved trauma, it can be difficult to see yourself for who you really are, and who you have always been.

Just as naming emotions or counting breaths in a mindfulness practice provides a focal point for the mind, writing-to-heal provides a focal point for awareness that allows for a meditative experience—one that can help rewire old, trauma-based neural pathways.

By putting pencil to paper, you're able to operate in the past, present, and future all at once. You engage in the present moment, even as your brain chooses words that call up events from the past. You create new meaning out of your experiences, which benefits you long into the future. And, you create a document that you can revisit in the future.

Revealing your story in words and learning to replace harmful, unreasonably negative thoughts with a more realistic and positive view of who you truly are calms the fear and arousal centers in the brain and helps to further the healing process. Creating a coherent narrative about what happened to you can help promote neural integration on a neurobiological level, which enhances feelings of resilience.

Take a moment to write about your current level of stress. **Do you feel you could benefit from having more tools to stay self-regulated, centered, and calm, especially when life feels overwhelming?**

_____

_____

_____

_____

_____

_____

Do you feel that you'd benefit from writing down your feelings as a means of developing more inner awareness? If so, how might this help you in your healing?

_____

_____

_____

_____

_____

How the Stress Cycle Works

> *A chronic state of being in fight, flight, freeze, or flop mode can change the setpoint for your well-being.*

We all know that emotional stress in our adult lives affects us on a physical level in quantifiable, life-altering ways. For instance, if you recently had an argument with your spouse, you're several times more likely to develop a cold in the next few days (Cohen et al. 2012).

When children or teens meet up with chronic adversity, it has an even more long-lasting impact. Inflammatory hormones and chemicals flood the developing brain and body, promoting a kind of low-brew, chronic inflammation that increases the likelihood of developing health challenges across a lifetime.

Why? When you face a potential threat or stressor or feel unsafe, you go into the first half of the stress cycle—fight, flight, freeze, or flop (flop refers to a fainting-like or feigning death–like state). You may experience an increase in heart rate, or feel butterflies in your stomach. Blood may rush into your arms and legs and away from your stomach and brain. You can't think well.

However, nature intended that after a stressor or threat has passed and as you begin to feel safe again, you enter the second half of the stress cycle—rest, digest, and relax. A sense of calm replaces fear.

Let's think about how your stress response is supposed to function in nature. Let's say you see a bear in the woods. Your body goes into fight, flight, freeze, or flop, and might prepare you to fight the bear or run from the bear, neither of which is a very good idea.

Let's say the bear isn't that interested in you and lumbers off. Now, your body goes through the second half of the stress cycle and relaxes, letting go of stress. *Ahhh.*

But what if the "bear" is in your home? What if the "bear" is a parent with a substance use disorder who comes home inebriated some nights and lashes out at you—but comes home on other nights and tells you he loves you? What if the "bear" is a parent who has an untreated mental health concern, who some days calls you stupid and other days hugs you and tells you she's proud of you?

What if you never know when the next bad moment is going to happen? When the "bear" is in the home, a child's developing body and brain never get to go through the second half of the stress cycle, into that normal, healthy state of relaxation.

When you grow up with *chronic unpredictable toxic stress*, and you never know when the next stressful event is coming, you get stuck in the first half of the stress cycle, living in a low-grade, constant state of alertness, hypervigilance—essentially a low-grade state of fight, flight, freeze, or flop.

As you consider these next questions, ask yourself if you're ready to answer them. If they bring up overwhelming emotions, you may need to skip them for now. Or, if helpful, return to a self-care exercise before answering them.

As a child or teen, what caused you to enter a state of fight, flight, or freeze?

Who or what was the source of stress in your story? Who was the "bear" in your home or life? (It might have been a parent, sibling, or grandparent with whom you did not always feel safe, or even an individual outside the home. Or it might be a circumstance, such as having a chronically ill parent, not enough food to eat, or living in a community that was unsafe.)

Does another "bear" (a person or circumstance that caused you to go into a state of alert) come to mind?

The Impact of Chronic Unpredictable Toxic Stress

You might be wondering how facing chronic unpredictable toxic stress (what I term CUTS) in childhood changes you on a physical level in ways that alter how well you're able to respond to and recover from stressors you may face today.

Over time, the inflammatory stress hormones and chemicals that the body pumps out in the face of threats and chronic unpredictable toxic stress cause epigenetic shifts to genes that oversee the stress response and how able you are to regulate your emotions. Yale researchers have shown that children who experienced adversity in childhood demonstrate changes to genes that oversee the stress response on all twenty-three chromosomes (Weder et al. 2014).

Studies have shown that the stress response can become stuck in the "on" position in children who face chronic unpredictable toxic stress. This can, over time, alter the setpoint for your well-being, leaving you in a chronic state of stress arousal.

This heightened stress response leads to increased production of inflammatory chemicals and stress hormones, which can lead to long-lasting shifts in the genes that oversee the stress response. This, in turn, can lead to increased inflammation, physical illness, and mental health concerns in adulthood, including anxiety and depression.

Reading this science can feel a little overwhelming at first. But it can also lead to new awareness as to how your past may live on in your body.

How does it feel to learn about this relationship between childhood adversity and your lifelong well-being?

How does this heightened stress response show up for you? When facing big stressors, do you have reactions or responses that you feel might be connected to having faced chronic unpredictable toxic stress as a child or teen?

🌿 Chronic Stress: What Can You Do?

If your brain receives the message that you will keep yourself safe, this communication helps to re-regulate your stress response in ways that help protect you and your mental and physical health.

As you notice your thoughts, you may observe that you are sending your brain non-stop danger-alert signals that increase the stress response, even as you want your brain and your immune system to function in as healthy a way as possible. It can be hard not to send these danger signals to yourself given all the challenges we face in today's world!

The goal is to help your body and brain—where trauma is lodged—to feel safe and calm as these experiences are noted and expressed, and to create the conditions where even though there has been an experience of chronic stress, trauma, or adversity, the brain can now rewire and begin to settle into a new felt-sense of well-being.

This program will help you begin to note the messages you are sending your brain and nervous system throughout your day, and begin to change them.

In the next exercise, we're going to delve deeper into the origins of your feelings of safety and unsafety in your childhood. By allowing these feelings to emerge, you will be better able to apply powerful new self-soothing techniques that can help rewire the brain for resiliency.

🌿 Draw Your Childhood Home

Now, let's gently dive into your own story.

Think about and draw the floor plan of your childhood home. Draw a rough floor plan of your primary home when you were growing up. If you moved around a lot or lived in more than one house, draw the floor plan of the home you most remember living in.

Now go in and add three to six details, such as the kitchen table where you had dinner with your family, or perhaps the closet where you kept your toys, or the front of the refrigerator. The more details the better. Do you remember the color of your closet door? How many chairs were at the dinner table? What photos or magnets might have been on the front of the refrigerator?

After you've added three to six details, add the front and back doors of the house and the yard, street, or sidewalk outside. Add two details about the outside of your childhood home.

By adding in details, such as how many chairs sat at the dining room table, where the snack cupboard was, or the location of a favorite tree outside your window, a variety of feelings and memories may have emerged for you. Some of these memories may be happy and fill you with a sense of safety and well-being. Others may be sad or bring up feelings of unsafety.

Again, before answering these next questions, take a moment to assess your nervous system. If needed, take a break, return to a self-soothing exercise, call a friend, or reach out to a trusted mental health practitioner.

What did daily life feel like for you growing up in your home?

Some locations might bring up feelings that are both happy and sad. That's perfectly normal too. Take a moment to reflect on the feelings that drawing your childhood floor plan brought up for you. **Simply jot these down now.**

Draw a Tree

Let's take another moment to put pen to paper by drawing a tree in the space pro-vided. I'd like you to think of this tree as loosely representing your life. It will help to follow these steps:

1. Draw a tree, any tree you like or feel called to draw. Whatever comes to you is fine—any size, shape, or type of tree.

2. Consider, as you draw, the tree's roots, trunk, limbs, and leaves.

3. Draw how far the tree branches out.

4. Imagine and draw the leaves.

5. Put gnarls or twisted or knotted parts in the tree trunk or branches—perhaps which speak to time periods of pain.

6. Color or shade in your drawing with a pencil or colored pencils.

Now let's take a moment and really look at the details of the tree you just drew. Sometimes you can find clues about your childhood experiences in this simple pencil and paper exercise.

For example, the tree I drew when I was in my twenties at the request of a therapist has a lower trunk that is thick and strong. The bark is protecting the tree.

But further up the trunk there is a large, gnarled area where there has clearly been some kind of injury, affecting how the tree grew.

Above this, many limbs stretch out toward the air and sun, and there is a light canopy of leaves. When I drew this a few decades ago, the therapist I was seeing looked at it and asked me, "What happened to you when you were twelve?" I looked at her in surprise, wondering how she could know that something significant had happened to me at that age. I told her, "When I was twelve, my father died suddenly from a medical error after undergoing a routine surgery."

She pointed to the gnarled area on the tree trunk. "In analyzing tree drawings, we think of this as a period of pre-adolescence," she said. "Clearly a major wound occurred here, something that changed how you grew after that time in your life."

She then talked about the limbs and the canopy of the tree and how the thin canopy of leaves I'd drawn demonstrated that I was still struggling to feel safe and protected and to achieve a state of post-traumatic growth and transformation.

I never forgot that experience, and since that time have redrawn my tree at different phases of my life, throughout my own healing journey, to see what comes up for me.

Over many years, even though my tree images still show gnarls in the trunk—that wound never disappears—my tree drawings show thicker, more robust limbs growing up and outward and a richer canopy of leaves rising up to meet the sun and light sheltering me.

Seeing the pattern that arises from our unconscious (when we draw our "tree") can help us gain insight into our own story.

Take a moment to listen to your thoughts and feelings about the tree you just drew and reflect on them.

Are there any areas of your tree that aren't healthy or strong? The trunk? The limbs? The growth of leaves? The roots?

_____

_____

_____

_____

_____

What memories, feelings, events, or emotional injuries do you think these areas on your tree represent?

_____

_____

_____

_____

_____

Which Self-Care Activities Resonate Most for You?

Think back to the breathing, mindfulness, and self-soothing exercises you've learned in this journal. Bear in mind that it can be hard to self-soothe if you were not soothed as a child. The capacity for self-soothing is born out of many instances of being soothed by someone else. If you faced a lot of adversity growing up, you might have become so adept at coping and surviving that you find it hard to tend to yourself now. Learning to do so can be like learning a new language. It may feel awkward or like hard work. That's okay. The rewards that come with learning this new language of self-tending are deep and long-lasting.

Take a moment to identify the activities you found the most calming. Write them here:

_____

_____

_____

_____

_____

_____

Remember, you can go back to this exercise at any time to help you re-center in body and mind. For additional mindfulness techniques to help you re-center in body and mind, please see the resources listed at the end of this book.

Part 3: Eleven Questions About Your Childhood

Every time I witness a strong person, I want to know:
What dark did you conquer in your story?
Mountains do not rise without earthquakes.
—Katherine MacKenett

Because children enter a fight-flight-freeze-flop state when trauma occurs, areas of the brain that manage and support the ability to verbalize feelings and think clearly in the moment shut down.

Now, I'm going to ask you to dive more deeply into some of your childhood experiences and memories and recall feelings you might have felt growing up. I want to reassure you that, having done this work with hundreds of individuals, it's very normal for powerful emotions to come up as we get deeper into this journal. You may find yourself feeling tearful or angry or overwhelmed. For others, what comes up is more of a felt-sense of unease or a tightness in the body.

I invite you to listen to what comes up for you, as you would listen to a friend, with that same loving, caring attention. If an exercise feels too overwhelming, please stop and take care of yourself, the same way you might take care of a friend who is recalling difficult memories or emotions. Take a walk, listen to music, or call a friend. Or reach out to a trusted mental health practitioner for support. Please also feel free to go back to the self-care practices you've learned.

I invite you to take these next few minutes to dive safely within—just for you and for no one else. Give yourself permission to fully participate in the exercise and set aside any resistance.

If a writing prompt does not apply to your experience, feel free to move on to the next one. Proceed at your own pace. Everyone is different. There is no right way to do these exercises.

Take an Emotional Leap

Let's start with eleven writing prompts that can help you take an emotional leap past your own resistance or feeling of not knowing where to begin. Set a timer for two minutes for writing each response. This will help you to capture your current stream of consciousness and responses without overthinking it. You will have a chance to revisit the writing prompts that resonate for you and write about them in more depth later. For this exercise, keep your hand moving. Write faster than you normally might, as if taking dictation from your mind as thoughts stream onto the page.

Here are a few important reminders as you begin this guided writing exercise:

· The exercises that follow do not require any special writing skills. Don't worry about writing your thoughts down in an organized way. You'll be engaging in expressive writing, which allows for free association, a quick discharge of your thoughts. These thoughts will later provide cues for you about key emotions that will be important as you continue through this journal, and on your path to healing.

· If you get stuck, simply look at the last sentence or two that you wrote. Choose a word and ask yourself, "What do I mean by ...?" This will help you keep going. Spend a moment before you begin this exercise to identify self-soothing techniques that you've enjoyed during this journal writing process. Utilize these when you need to take a break to help ground yourself.

- Again, consider taking breaks and checking in to share what you wrote with a trusted friend, partner, or practitioner.

1. **In what place might you have felt safe as a child?** Perhaps your bedroom, your grandparents' home, a friend's house, or a tree in the backyard.

2. **Did people in your home seem to enjoy each other's company? How so, or not so?**

3. Where did you go when you were upset as a child? Did you have someone to turn to for comfort? How did you try to soothe yourself?

_____

_____

_____

_____

_____

4. What was the hardest year or period of years during your childhood? How old were you then? What happened during that time?

_____

_____

_____

_____

_____

5. What happened in your family that made you feel emotionally left out, or ignored, or not important? This might include the behavior of parents, caregivers, siblings, or family dynamics.

6. When might you have been physically abandoned or left behind? This might include being separated from your parents, or the death of a parent or loved one, or parents separating or divorcing, or being in foster care, or adopted.

7. How or when did you feel verbally or emotionally shamed, diminished, blamed, discounted, disregarded, or humiliated?

8. When might you have witnessed siblings, a parent, or a caregiver being put down or made fun of, or verbally humiliated?

9. When might you have been made to feel you had to care for others in order to be loved or feel safe?

_____

_____

_____

_____

_____

10. What happened as a child that you had difficulty articulating or talking about to your parents, caregivers, or grownups back then, when it happened—or perhaps have had difficulty talking about to anyone since?

_____

_____

_____

_____

_____

11. What did you want from your mother or father that you never received?

_____

_____

_____

_____

_____

Bring in your earlier image, imagining yourself as an infant, and that you are the loving parent to that child you once were. Imagine being the mother or father who sees and instantly recognizes the beauty and the miracle of who you are and who you have always been.

Hold this image in your mind's eye, and now imagine bringing this image into your heart.

If heavy emotions are coming up, acknowledge that your younger self—the inner child within you—is feeling overwhelmed, uncertain, wanting to know what to do next in order to feel safe.

Soothe that young child and tell them, "It's okay, we're going to get there, it's okay to simply be right now, and rest in this growing feeling of relaxation, of safety that comes with being on a healing path."

 Explicit and Implicit Memories

It's okay if you can't recall specific memories. Often when you have a history of trauma, it's hard to recall specific details of events. It might just be a general feeling (sadness, fear, anger, loss) that arises.

Explicit memories

Some trauma memories are lodged in regions of the brain that are accessible via words, visual memory, verbalizing them on paper, or speaking them aloud. When you think about them, you might recall visual details or emotions as if a movie scene were playing out in your mind. We call these movie scene-like memories *explicit* memories.

Implicit Memories

Some trauma experiences are not accessible. You may only have a felt sense of what you experienced. It may be hard to bring words or images to describe what happened. You might not remember or know details. These traumatic experiences often come up as unpleasant sensations, feelings, emotions, thoughts, a sense of general anxiety or discomfort, or unwelcome bodily sensations (tightness, pressure, discomfort, contraction, heaviness, nausea, pain). We call these somatic experiences.

We call these nonverbal memories and "felt-sense" emotions *implicit memories*. They can either stay below the level of conscious awareness or appear as flashbacks (which one may or may not recognize as coming from the past).

Identifying Sticky Memories

For this exercise, you will need to have a marker on hand. When you have finished writing, we are going to go back and look at what you wrote. You will use your marker to circle and underline anything you wrote that has deep emotional resonance for you: whatever feels most "sticky" or "heated."

I invite you to look back over your answers to the previous questions and the feelings you wrote about. I'd like you to look for "sticky feelings," those old, familiar feelings that we find ourselves getting stuck in when they come up. Often, it's hard to let them go.

We might also think of these sticky feelings as "white hot" moments of experience. Things that still feel heated and overwhelming when you think about them now, even years later.

As you look over your answers to the questions about your childhood, what experiences or feelings still bring up the most "emotional heat?" These might be moments when you felt the most unsafe, scared, or unsure of what was happening.

_____

_____

_____

_____

_____

Now go back with a marker and underline anything you wrote in the answer above that has deep emotional resonance for you: whatever feels most "sticky" or "heated."

Hiraeth n. A Welsh word for homesickness or nostalgia, an earnest longing or desire or a sense of regret. A homesickness for a home to which you cannot return, a home that maybe never was; the nostalgia, the yearning, the grief for the lost places of your past.

Self-Care Activity: Take in a Heart Breath

In this meditation, you will check in with your body and take in a heart breath.

Instructions

Please find a comfortable place to sit or lie down. Either is fine.

To begin, gently close your eyes. See if you can go inside and notice what is happening in your body after writing about these feelings and experiences.

Where do you feel that fear or anger or loss in your body?

If you were to glance in a mirror, what would your facial expression reflect back to you about how you are feeling right now?

Notice your jaw, your shoulders, your heart space, your belly. Follow your breath. Inhale and let out a slow exhale.

It's okay if you can't locate a sensation. If you do feel a sense of bodily tension, bring your awareness to that tightness.

Ask yourself if you can gently soften around the edges of that tightness. Offer a soothing light all around the edges of it.

Now, let's take in a few heart breaths.

Place your hands over your heart, one over the other. Breathe in from the soles of your feet, up from the center of the earth, as you simultaneously breathe in to the crown of your head from the sky. Imagine holding this healing breath in all four chambers of your heart.

Then slowly exhale. Imagine your exhale extending out horizontally from the front and back of your heart.

Take another heart breath in, and as you breathe out, see if you can release any tension.

Write Down Your Sticky Phrases

Write down the sticky phrases you circled and underlined when identifying sticky memories that had the most emotional resonance for you:

Circle and underline these phrases again.

I invite you to get creative. You might want to draw stars, exclamations, lightning bolts, or other images around these "sticky" phrases to emphasize how they stood out to you in terms of your own story.

Part 4: Finding Your Benefactors

You may not control all the events that happen to you,
but you can decide not to be reduced by them.
—Maya Angelou

Please get out the photos you gathered of those significant people who have loved or mentored you, or with whom you have felt safe and loved. These might be someone who is living or deceased. They might be a loving adult, friend, pet, or even a spiritual figure. If you don't have access to any photos, that's okay too. You can simply imagine them and hold these images in your mind.

We call these allies from our past and present our benefactors. Most of us know who our benefactors are because of how they made us feel when we were with them. We felt safe, seen, known, and secure when we were in their presence. We felt loved.

Benefactors are simply trusted adults or spiritual beings with whom we feel understood, valued, and supported for exactly who we are. They often stand out in our memory and bring up warm emotions because they were so loving and supportive. Perhaps they knew how to comfort and console us. When we were with them, we felt special, safe, and protected. Perhaps we no longer felt helpless, lonely, or afraid.

Our benefactors may have also offered us good counsel, said words of encouragement, or let us know they believed in us, with words we still recall and draw on today.

I have a deeply felt sense that my benefactors have helped me in many ways to survive, even to thrive, during the most difficult years of my life. I often find myself wanting to emulate their inner strengths.

> *We know who our benefactors are because of how they made us feel when we're with them: we felt safe, seen, known, secure when we were in their presence. We felt loved.*

I have a picture of my father and me when I was nine years old. It was taken on Christmas Eve. He would die just a few years later when I was twelve. When I was with my dad, I felt a true sense of safety and comfort. My father was also a writer and a journalist. He was a newspaper editor. When I was very young, he instilled in me a sense of love and an affinity for the written word. We used to read poetry together, such as Robert Louis Stevenson and Robert Frost. And before he died, he gave me his collected works of Shakespeare. I still think of my dad every day, and when I'm feeling overwhelmed, unsafe, or unsure, I often draw upon the sense of safety that I felt when I was with him.

Inviting in Your Benefactors

Drawing upon our internal resources by calling in benefactors—whether real or imagined—can help to stimulate an interior sense of being loved, of being safe, of secure attachment, which can help promote healthier neural pathways and neural connections.

In this exercise, I invite you to imagine and invite a circle of your benefactors to sit with you right here, right now. This might be one person or being, or it might be several people or beings.

Who is here with you?

_____

_____

_____

_____

How do you feel when you imagine being in their presence—a positive sense of safety, an interior light, a sense of possibility, or a feeling of interior flourishing or inner strength?

_____

_____

_____

_____

Imagine each of your benefactors putting their hands over your hands or holding you—whatever feels most comfortable to you—as they extend their love to you. **How do they make you feel?**

_____

_____

_____

_____

_____

_____

_____

_____

Breathe in their love, their presence. Feel that sense of safety expand throughout your body and your heart.

Recall a Recent Stressful Situation or Interaction

Take a few minutes to recall a recent time or situation in your life in which you had big, overwhelming feelings and might have overreacted, or shut down. Perhaps you "flipped your lid."

_____

_____

_____

_____

_____

We can recognize these moments in retrospect because these are often scenarios in which we later wish we'd behaved "better" or differently, or "said the right thing." We often keep replaying them in our minds—what was said, what wasn't said, how we felt.

When you think about a recent stressful situation or encounter in your life, do you find yourself wishing you had reacted differently or said or done something differently?

If so, how?

_____

_____

_____

_____

Perhaps your moment of big feelings wasn't anything you displayed to anyone else, but it was a lashing out at yourself over something you felt you should have done better, or differently, and you found yourself caught up in ruminating with intense feelings of regret, self-recrimination, shame, or guilt. **When you think about this recent, stressful situation or interaction, did you turn on yourself with self-blame or self-criticism?**

If so, how?

_____

_____

_____

_____

Let's look more closely at these big, overwhelming moments, and what triggers you in your present life. **When are you most likely to "lose it," lash out at yourself, or disappear?**

_____

_____

_____

_____

When you think back over this recent interaction or incident, where were you, who was there, how did you feel, why did you feel this way?

_____

_____

_____

_____

_____

What did you need, but not receive? From others? From yourself? Go ahead and touch into that anger, loss, sadness, or agitation.

_____

_____

_____

_____

Take a deep breath. Let it go. If helpful, ask your benefactors to sit with you as you allow your feelings to emerge.

Now, look over what you've written, and let's go back, using your marker, and circle and underline the words, emotions, or phrases that bring forth the most intense sensations or the "stickiest" feelings for you.

Returning to Your Sticky Feelings from Childhood

Now, I want to invite you to go back in time again to your childhood and teenage years and reflect on some of your stickiest feelings, memories, and emotions from the past.

At the same time, I'd like you to also bear in mind everything you just wrote in the last exercise, when you recalled a recent scenario in which you felt overwhelmed by big emotions.

1. **Was this recent scenario the first time you've ever felt these emotions and feelings?** Without overthinking it, just notice what emerges. Be curious.

2. **Do these feelings or reactions have anything in common with similar big feelings you had as a child, an adolescent, or as a young adult?** Write about any ways in which your recent reactions or overwhelming feelings feel similar to those you experienced when you were young.

3. Know it's okay if nothing specific comes up at first, or at all. Just stay curious. A specific scenario from when you were younger may emerge.

_____

_____

_____

_____

_____

Or, when you think about that time growing up when you had similar big feelings, you might have a general sense of how you felt as a child or a teenager—a sense of physical heaviness, tightness, or sense of tension.

_____

_____

_____

_____

4. Stay with that image or thought about that earlier time in your life. If a specific memory does come to mind, write about it here.

_____

_____

_____

_____

_____

5. Now, let's go a little deeper. What is that younger version of yourself feeling?

_____

_____

_____

_____

_____

6. What do you imagine that young child within, your inner child, is unconsciously believing to be true about themselves?

7. Ask that younger version of yourself: What are they telling themself about themself during this earlier scenario when they were a child or teenager?

Often this is some version of, "I'm not okay, I'm not capable, good enough, smart enough. I'm not lovable. It's my fault. I'm a bad person. I'm inadequate. I'm ugly or my body is hateful. I did something wrong or I have to work harder. Things will never be easier. I do not deserve love."

8. Write for the next two minutes about what is coming up for you.

9. **What became your inner child's "truth" at a young age?**

Yours may be something like: "Something's wrong with me. I'm not lovable. I'm not worthy. I'm not supposed to be here. I'll never amount to anything." Or it may be, "I can't trust anyone, people take advantage of me." or "My feelings don't matter. I don't matter."

_____

_____

_____

_____

_____

What comes up for you could be a sense of wordless dread. You may not be able to describe it in words. You may experience a sense of shame, rejection, feeling unworthy, or a sense that you are not "at home" within yourself. A feeling that you are not good enough in your relationships, as a parent, or as a person.

Pay attention to phrases and feelings that convey a sense of unworthiness.

10. **Were there ways in which you had to be or behave in order to stay safe or have your needs met?**

    Examples of statements reflecting this situation: "I will be good. I will not have needs. I won't ever ask for help. I will try to meet the needs of others. I have to stay small to stay safe." Or it could sound like, "I have to look out for myself. I have to be bigger than life, push my way through, do whatever it takes." Or you may think, "I have to work harder than anyone else. If I just keep trying harder, I will be okay."

    _____

    _____

    _____

    _____

11. **If feelings are coming up for you, name them and write them down as you experience them—whether sadness, grief, fear, regret, anger, anxiousness, etc.**

    _____

    _____

    _____

    _____

12. **Continue to write about these feelings. When you are finished, we'll look back at what you've written and see what feelings and emotions stand out for you the most.**

_____

_____

_____

_____

_____

_____

_____

_____

_____

Now let's go back and circle and underline the words, emotions, or phrases that resonate the most and bring forth the "stickiest" feelings, feelings that bring up the most "heat" when you think about what that younger part of yourself believed about herself.

Connecting the Dots

I'd like you to take a look at everything you've written and circled throughout this book. List the emotions that came up for you in the past and those that came up in your present life and compare them side by side. This will help you to easily see the parallels between feelings and emotions that arose in the past and those that arise for you now.

Emotions and "sticky" thoughts past	Emotions and "sticky" thoughts present

Look at the emotions and statements you wrote above. **Do any of the emotions and "sticky" emotions and thoughts from your past resonate with how you felt in a recent moment when you were overwhelmed? Are they similar? How so?**

_____

_____

_____

_____

If in your present life scenario your feelings were hurt, you might notice that something feels familiar about that. For example, upon closer inspection, you may notice that in the more recent scenario you felt shamed, belittled, ignored, or insulted, just as you did when you were small. You may have felt a sense of familiar unworthiness.

What parallels do you see between the messages that your younger self began to believe about who you are and how you felt in your more recent scenario or situation?

What early beliefs you are still carrying?

What might be under this? What are the similarities or patterns in these situations today and those in the past when you felt most unseen, neglected, afraid, unsafe, hurt, or unvalued?

_____

_____

_____

_____

_____

Self-Care Activity: Vagal Nurturing

Vagal nurturing is another powerful self-soothing technique. This exercise, developed by Marti Glenn, PhD, can help you to calm your nervous system and reset your stress response in just two minutes.

Instructions

To begin, gently close your eyes. Notice what is happening in your body just now. Check your belly, your heart space, your breath. Scan your whole body. Just noticing.

Now, place both feet on the floor.

When you do each of the steps below, you will take a breath and focus on your slow exhale, making your exhale longer than the inhale. This gives maximum stimulation for the vagus nerve.

Take a breath in. As you breathe in, place one hand on each ear and gently pull the outer part of your ears, beginning at the bottom of your ears, moving up. As you finish pulling on your ears, let out a long exhale.

Move the flat palms of your hands to comfortably cover your eyes. Remember playing hide-and-seek as a kid? You will probably find the base of your hands resting on your cheekbones. Inhale, and let out a nice, slow exhale.

Slide your hands down and cup your hands under your chin and jaws as if cupping the face of a precious child. See if you can imagine a person who loves you holding your face in their hands. This could be someone from your past, someone you know now, or someone you imagine in your future. The base of your hands will be resting under your chin, your thumbs close to your jawbone. Inhale, and let out a slow exhale.

Slide your hands down either side of your neck and place them, one on top of each other, over your heart. As you inhale, you will feel a nice, firm pressure beneath your hands. Now, let out a long, slow exhale.

Slide your hands along the sides of your body, down over your ribs, and place them, one on top of the other, over your belly. As you inhale, you will feel a nice, firm pressure under your hands. Now let out a long exhale.

Leave one hand on your belly and move the top hand back up to the heart. Inhale. Just like before, notice what this feels like as you focus on your long exhale.

As you are ready, inhale, and open your eyes and open your arms. You may rest your arms, palms open, on your lap or wherever is most comfortable. Imagine a positive word or phrase coming to you as you continue breathing. Sometimes people hear things such as, "I can do this" or "I believe in myself" or "You are loved."

Whatever positive thoughts come, just sit with them.

When you are finished, write down any phrases that come to you.

Part 5: Naming Your Feelings

In the brain, naming an emotion can help calm it . . . finding
words to label an internal experience becomes really helpful.
—Dan Siegel, MD

Old beliefs get wired and fired into your neurocircuitry, influencing how you respond today.

Often, how you felt in past moments and encounters can shape or interfere with your sense of who you are now, the sense of "me" that you still carry.

These old beliefs are most likely to come up when you feel overwhelmed by events around you, when there is a lot of chaos in your life, or when others are behaving in ways that feel hurtful or make you feel unsafe.

> *We often think of all of these stressors as occurring in the world around us. But sometimes, the most stressful messages you receive are the ones you send to yourself.*

When you enter a fight, flight, freeze, or flop state, areas of the brain that are associated with logic, reason, and verbalizing your feelings go offline. When we feel unsafe or perceive threats in our environment, the brain isn't really concerned with logic or finding just the right words. The brain is more concerned with the danger you may be in.

Studies show that naming your feelings with specific words—what we call emotional granulation—helps with emotional regulation (Torre and Lieberman 2018). Doing so gives you a mental pause to figure out the best way to handle your feelings, while also calming down your nervous system.

And the more specific you are about your emotions and naming them—both of which require taking an action that breaks your state of rumination—the more the nervous system settles down. Writing out your feelings is an action that can help you to break the rumination cycle.

Ruminating thoughts are thoughts in which we repetitively think about a negative or unpleasant experience, or worry about events in the future. These often show up in daily life as judging ourselves or others. For instance, after a difficult interaction with someone you care about, or after you've made a mistake, you might find yourself riddled with self-criticism and self-doubt:

I'm an idiot. How could I do that? I ruined everything. Was I too harsh? Maybe I should apologize. I'm an awful person/spouse/ mother. I said too much. I should have stood up for myself more! I always say the wrong thing. I'm such a loser. Here's what I'll say next time.

Or, you might find yourself caught up in judging others harshly or harboring grievances with others, focusing on how they wronged you. *They always make fun of me. How could they not listen to what I have to say? No one listens. I don't matter to people. I'll never trust them again. They're horrible. What they did was unforgivable. What a jerk!*

🌿 Old Thought Cycles

You might be wondering what your old thought cycles look like, the ones that you learned during times of adversity and trauma. As you learned earlier, when you have a history of adverse childhood experiences and trauma, you may become limited in your ability to respond to new stressors in your life appropriately. This might look like any of the following:

- Overreacting when encountering frustration, being criticized, being ignored

- Feeling lonely when trying to connect with others

- Isolating in order to protect yourself from interactions with others

- Avoiding contradicting or disagreeing with others in order to prevent hurting their feelings

- Saying yes because saying no might hurt someone's feelings

- "Fawning" or over-complimenting others out of a need to please

- Needing and even demanding attention from others

- Overachievement or being highly competitive even over small things

- Pursuing perfection over small details

- General feelings of dissatisfaction, chronic judging, or blaming of yourself or others

- Feeling you lack empathic feelings when others are facing hardships or struggles

- Difficulty in voicing important emotions or needs

- Compulsive caretaking, helping others instead of yourself

- Focusing on others' pain instead of your own pain, needs, and feelings

Many of these are strategies you might have needed to employ when you were growing up in order to make it through very difficult times. When you were a child, they might have served you well to get through traumatic situations. But in adult life, they are no longer helpful adaptive strategies.

Think for a moment about your own ruminating thought patterns. **When you make a mistake, regret something, or feel hurt, are there familiar phrases or thoughts of self-criticism, or blaming others, that tend to arise in your mind? What are these thought patterns?** (It can help to imagine these thoughts like a radio station playing in the background. What is your radio station saying?)

Examples of Thought Cycles

It can be very hard to escape your old thought patterns and cycles of rumination when you're triggered by stressful events that bring up overwhelming feelings in your adult life. This is especially true for individuals who've experienced trauma and adversity growing up. Here are some examples of ruminating thought cycles:

- A therapist became triggered and caught up in ruminating thought cycles when overwhelmed by caring for her children and husband, especially when no one in her family was helping her. This dynamic brought up similar feelings of having to take care of her parents' emotional needs from the time she was very young—or what's known as "parentification"—without having anyone to rely on or turn to. "No one ever helps me, they don't care about what I need, I'm always on my own."

- A physician became triggered and caught up in ruminating thought cycles when his wife was busy with their children's lives and needs and had little time for him. This dynamic brought up similar feelings of abandonment from when he was a child. His parents, both surgeons, were rarely home—and he would watch the taillights of their cars as they left the driveway from his bedroom window. "My biggest memory is always seeing the taillights of the car leaving the driveway...being left alone."

- An advocate was triggered when taken advantage of by colleagues who utilized her work without credit or didn't listen to her ideas in meetings. Their actions brought up similar feelings of helplessness, rage, and needs being ignored when she was seventeen and was sexually abused by an older stepbrother. "Everyone takes advantage, diminishes me, bullies, and forces what they want onto me."

- An event planner whose mother died when she was sixteen became triggered whenever she faced problems at work or in her personal life that she didn't know how to solve. This brought up old feelings of inadequacy because she hadn't known how to help her mom when her mom was ill.

When you read these examples, what old thought patterns of your own come to mind?

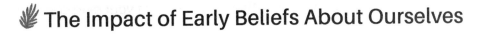 The Impact of Early Beliefs About Ourselves

Think about the recent upsetting situation you recalled in part 4. More than likely, an old belief got activated in that moment. These beliefs can color the lens through which you see the world, distorting your interpretations and perceptions of what is happening around you. The old beliefs keep you on guard, blocking your potential to be who and how you want to be in your relationships, at work, as a parent—and in your relationship with yourself.

Simply noting this connection can help you to recognize those moments when they are happening, which, in turn, can help you to soothe yourself. When you become aware of these links between past and present "sticky" moments, the revelation in and of itself is self-regulating, helping you to be able to better flourish in the moment, even in the face of adversity. This helps us to increase what we call our window of tolerance, or our window of presence in the face of life's inevitable challenges.

Think about the recent upsetting situation you wrote about in part 4. **As you recall this scenario, what thought patterns become activated?**

How might these feelings and thought patterns have been colored by old beliefs you still carry about yourself?

What feelings and thoughts feel the "oldest" and most familiar?

 ## Self-Regulation

When you're triggered or overwhelmed by old feelings and beliefs, you're also more likely to overreact or underreact. You may find that you're not "home" in your body. You "disappear."

When you have "big feelings," you probably find that you go above or below your window of tolerance and are no longer present. When you are under-regulated, you may lash out. When you are over-regulated, you may keep it all in and resent others.

You may engage in judging, shaming, or blaming yourself and others. The goal is to have the capacity to stay cool, calm, present, aware, and connected most of the time. This is our safe space.

Does this sound familiar to you? How so?

If you find yourself wishing you had a greater capacity to stay cool, calm, present, and connected during difficult interactions, is there a particular person or relationship in your life in which this is often the case? If so, whom?

Is there a particular environment in which you wish you had a greater capacity to stay calm and present? (It might be at work, when visiting your parents, or with a particular friend group.) If so, where?

Now, let's work on how to name difficult feelings with emotional granulation.

Learning how to name our most difficult feelings in detail can be an important step in changing the way in which we talk to ourselves. As you learn to name your emotions and feelings, which might include anger, fear, shame, sadness, grief, or dread, please do it with a sense of love for the child you once were, and for how brave you were to deal with these feelings on your own. As you write, note any physical sensations that arise, such as a pounding heart, or a weight on your chest.

Here are a few examples of emotional granulation:

- The therapist whose story we read about earlier came up with an emotionally granular phrase for when no one was helping her—her teenagers were sleeping in late and the kitchen was a mess with dishes everywhere. Her phrase was: "No-one-helps-me-seething-chest!"

- The physician who was triggered when his wife became busy and wrapped up in their children came up with this phrase: "Lonely-heart-pounding abandonment."

- The advocate who was triggered when taken advantage of by colleagues came up with this phrase: "Familiar-fury-blast-of-unsafety."

- The event planner whose mother died when she was sixteen came up with this phrase: "Heart-dread-of-unfixable-loss."

I encourage you to look back through your book and revisit the old thought patterns and stories that emerged when you were a child or teenager and pay special attention to the feelings that you circled. **Now, take a moment to choose a few words that describe your oldest feelings and emotions.**

And a few words that describe your oldest physical sensations.

Now, let's combine your oldest feelings and emotions and your oldest physical sensations to make a single *mind–body phrase* that reflects how you felt (and still feel) during times of heightened adversity. A mind–body phrase is a term that encompasses your emotional and physical states. I've included one of my own to get you started.

In my own healing journey, I've found that my stickiest feelings emerge when I feel no one cares about my welfare or feelings, that I don't matter, even as I take care of others' needs and emotions. This emerges from having lost my father when I was a child and having to care for the emotional needs of my widowed mother, who was suffering greatly. When these feelings are triggered, they bring up very old emotions and physical sensations. For example:

Old emotion:	Old physical sensation:	Your mind–body phrase:
My feelings don't matter to anyone.	*Shallow breath and tight chest.*	*I never matter, can't breathe chest.*

You might want to try a few different combinations of old emotions and old physical sensations to see which mind–body phrase (or phrases) resonates most for you. Please give it a try:

Old emotion:	Old physical sensation:	Your mind–body phrase:

Old emotion:	Old physical sensation:	Your mind–body phrase:

Old emotion:	Old physical sensation:	Your mind–body phrase:

In sum, your mind–body phrase is a combination of words you choose to describe and name your emotional, mind–body state when old feelings from childhood feel similar to, or resonate with, current overwhelming feelings in adult life. You can use it in difficult situations and moments to (silently, in your own mind) name your difficult emotions and feelings so that you're better able to step back from big feelings, recognize they are emerging from old wounds, and return to the present with a greater capacity to be compassionate and caring to yourself, and to others, while staying calm and present.

Self-Care Activity: Releasing and Letting Go of Tension

To begin: Take in a deep breath to the count of 6, hold for the count of 4, and release slowly to the count of 7.

We're going to go through a series of three brief exercises using your imagination to visualize letting go of and releasing any tension you may be feeling.

If you feel areas of tightness in any part of your body—perhaps your neck, your shoulders, your head, or your chestcplace your attention on that area and imagine there are bands tied around it. Now imagine that these bands are being slowly untied. As they loosen and begin to fall away, all of your tension eases.

Here is a second brief visualization exercise. Go back to any area of your body where you may be holding tension, perhaps your neck or your shoulders. Now imagine, if you can, that there are little ice skating–like figures moving around in that muscle or area, skating around, loosening and breaking down any muscle tightness.

Here is a third visualization exercise. Imagine you're sitting in the deep sea, watching the fish float by, the waving sea fans, the penetrating rays of sun striking the sea coral in an array of glorious colors all around you. Just watch the sea life go by and feel all the tension from your body let go.

If you noticed areas of tightness or tension in your body while doing these exercises, where were they?

Is this often where you hold tension in your body?

Which, if any, of the above visualizations helped you to let go and relax?

Where did you feel yourself letting go of anxiety or tension?

Now ask yourself what might happen if, whenever you feel overwhelmed in your current life, you were able to note and name the old feelings and emotions + old physical sensations—your trauma mind-body phrase—that you identified during this lesson while combining this noting and naming with one of the above mindfulness techniques. **Do you feel it might help you to relax and feel calmer and more present during difficult situations?**

_____

_____

_____

_____

_____

Give it a try the next time you're feeling overwhelmed simply name your trauma mind-body phrase to note your experience, then practice using whichever visualization exercise resonates most for you.

When you are engaging in the process of neural re-narrating, there is a great deal of power in hearing yourself say things out loud. Consider sharing your trauma mind-body phrase with a friend or partner, and, if it feels safe to do so, tell them why you chose the words you did. Or, read your trauma mind-body phrase aloud to yourself.

 # "Hello Brain"

Throughout every day, there are messages you send your brain. Let's look at these with curiosity. As you go through your day, take this journal along with you and make note of the messages you send yourself.

- **ASK:** Throughout your day, ask yourself these questions: "Hello Brain: What messages am I sending you right now about who we are? About whether we are safe or not safe? Good or not good? Worthy or not worthy?" **Write down what arises:**

- **LOOK:** Look with curiosity at what messages come up for you most often. **Write down what you notice:**

- **REPEAT:** When you are next triggered in your present life, repeat your old feelings and emotions + old physical sensations—or trauma mind–body phrase—to yourself as you bring in one of the self-care, breath, or mindfulness practices you have learned so far in this book. **How did that feel for you?**

- **PAUSE:** See if by doing so you can pause for several breaths before you respond to any given situation in which you feel overwhelmed or triggered. **Which self-care practice did you choose?**

_____

_____

_____

_____

_____

How did that feel for you?

_____

_____

_____

_____

_____

- **AWARENESS:** If you notice or feel agitated that you're falling into old, reactive patterns in how you respond, think, feel, or react when triggered, know that simply having the awareness that you've fallen back into an old pattern is a tremendous sign of your hard-won progress and of your determination to wake up on your own side. That self-realization is a powerful and important stepping stone in the path to healing and transformation. **Take a moment here to thank yourself for doing this work. Write a few words of appreciation—to yourself—for your efforts:**

Part 6: Learning the Power of Kind Self-Talk

Don't BeLittle Yourself, BeBig Yourself.
—Marti Glenn, PhD

Your brain works a lot like a computer system taking in all the input it gets, including the messages that you send your brain. Your habits of self-talk and beliefs about yourself are like the software program that your brain runs on.

Both your brain and body are deeply influenced by the quality of how you talk to yourself. The things you say to yourself, how you feel about yourself, are like a computer code, which sends instructions every millisecond to your body in ways that have a powerful impact on your overall sense of well-being.

Your self-talk can either increase your level of stress, anxiety, and feelings of being overwhelmed, or ease your level of stress and help create a sense of inner well-being and flourishing. As previously mentioned, one way of thinking about this is to imagine that your self-talk is like a radio station you have playing all the time in the background.

The things you say to yourself, how you feel about yourself are like a computer code, which send instructions every milli-second to your body in ways that have a powerful impact on your overall sense of well-being.

If you are dialed into what I think of as the pain channel and are frequently sending negative self-talk messages to yourself, over time, that is going to keep you caught up in a state of low-grade fight-flight-freeze-flop. This, in turn, can generate chronic inflammation in both body and brain.

If you are dialed in, instead, to what I call the life channel and you're able to reflect on the good that's within you and see the positive ways in which you interact with the world around you, that's going to harness the neurobiological anti-inflammatory power of the mind–body connection.

Throughout this book, you've learned to notice the messages of self-criticism and unworthiness that you send yourself. When you think about those negative messages and self-talk, how do you feel about the way you talk to yourself? (This might include feelings like, "I want to be kinder to myself." Or, "I wish I weren't so hard on myself." Or, "I feel sad that I'm always beating up on myself.") **Write about what comes up for you:**

What messages would you like to stop sending yourself? (This might include self-talk such as, "I'm such an idiot." Or, "I always do X." Or, "Of course I messed up." Or, "I'm a terrible mother.") **Write down the self-talk habits you'd like to break:**

Your Brain as Detective

Your brain reacts to stress, adversity, and uncertainty based on your unconscious habitual patterns. Your brain is like a detective on the lookout for clues and evidence that will align with your old beliefs, thought patterns, and perspectives. If your core belief about your inner self is that you are not good enough, or lacking, your brain will constantly search for ways to prove this belief to you.

You can help the brain shift its habitual response from searching for what is "wrong with you" to searching for and reminding yourself of positive self-truths about yourself. When we interrupt our habitual reactions many times throughout the day and take new actions by utilizing new resources—such as those we are learning in this book—we begin to create the conditions for interior flourishing.

It's important to stop, pause, listen to these messages and approach them with curiosity. Ask yourself: What is my brain trying to prove to me is true about me/my world right now? Is that message serving me?

The goal is to reset the mission directives: Give your brain-as-detective a more helpful and beneficial job—to search out and reaffirm the good, eternal truths about yourself that have always been there.

Positive Self-Messaging

In this next exercise, we're going to draw on internal resources for learning new, more positive self-messaging.

You will also be using your imagination in positive ways to activate brain cells known as "mirror neurons," which can help your brain to imitate the images that you put in front of it in ways that can help create healthier neural pathways for flourishing.

Instructions

Take out the photos you set aside as you began this journal and choose one or several photos of yourself at a young age.

Place the photo, or several photos, in front of you.

If you don't have access to any photos of your younger self, simply imagine a photo that you've seen of yourself when you were young and hold that in your mind.

Invite your loving adult self—who you are right now—to comfort your inner child within.

Sit with and comfort and cradle that younger child. Tell that younger self, "I'm here."

From this vantage point, is it true that the younger version of you is not capable, or is not lovable, or is unworthy?

Get a sense of that precious inner child, the innocence, the sweetness of them. What is the truth about your younger self? Is that younger you good, kind, smart, well-intentioned, lovable?

_____

_____

_____

If it feels comfortable for you, close your eyes.

Ask your benefactors to join you.

Ask them to tell that young child within the truth about your younger self.

They might remind you of acts of kindness you offered others, how you loved and tried to help those around you. They might remind you of your child's heart of longing or compassion, of efforts you made on your own behalf that required courage and fortitude, or perhaps times you found strength and resilience when you thought you couldn't go on.

What have your benefactors shared with you about your interior goodness and who you truly are?

_____

_____

_____

Take in that TRUTH.

Now open your eyes.

Looking back, think of a time or a memory when you were facing challenges as a child. Think about how hard your younger self tried. See if you can smile at and admire that young child, trying so hard to do what they needed to do to be loved, even in the face of adversity—perhaps without having the loving adult support she needed at the time. **Write about that time.**

How would you describe this younger self? Persistent? Caring? Loving? Resilient? **Write down positive adjectives and good qualities about your younger self.**

As you write these down, tell your younger self that you know how lovable and good and worthy she is. You know. You see that in her. **What does it feel like to go back in time and tell that child you see their worthiness, that they matter, and that they belong?**

_____

_____

_____

_____

_____

_____

Now let's bring in an older, wiser image of yourself—a decade older than you are now. Imagine the three of you sitting together: your older, wiser self; the you you are now; and your younger self. Imagine your older, wiser self is smiling at your smiling, as you recognize the core truths about your essential goodness and worthiness.

Continue to imagine your older, wiser self smiling at you, and smiling at your younger self, as you continue to smile at your younger self.

You might lift the corners of your lips in a slight smile as you do this exercise. And even allow your eyes to smile.

Imagine all of these "selves" are sitting together in a safe place—a bench in the park, on a dock, on a rock overlooking a beautiful mountain view.

Take in the beauty around you. Marinate in these good feelings.

Now look back at the positive adjectives you used to describe your younger self. The truth about your inner child.

Circle the words that resonate the most.

Write your TRUTH about who you have always been. (This might be, "I will always care for and keep myself safe." Or, "I am filled with essential goodness and always have been." Or, "I love and am loved." Or, "I am resilient and persist even when things are hard.")

_____

_____

_____

_____

_____

_____

_____

_____

_____

_____

_____

Write your truth on Post-it notes in places where you will see them often. At home on the fridge, on your computer, in your car. On the back of your smartphone.

Use these to remind yourself of your TRUTH.

🌿 Powerful Tools to Change Your Self-Talk

Now, let's look at the neural power of self-talk. You're going to use your own name as you invite your older, wiser self to talk to you as a best friend or benefactor might. Shifting from saying "I" to referring to yourself in the third person by using your own name increases powerful self-regulatory effects in the brain.

We usually talk to ourselves in the third person to say or think negative things about ourselves! For example, when driving, we might say: "_____, you missed the turn, you idiot!"

We rarely talk to ourselves in the third person in positive ways. For example, we could say:

_____, *you are caring, loving, and resilient.*

_____, *you are good. Lovable. Capable.*

Talking to ourselves in the third person in positive ways helps fire and wire new synapses in the brain. Whatever your truth is, it is yours. It is important that your truth be in your language, your words. Say it to yourself several times a day.

What we're looking for here is much more than words or knowing. We are looking for an experience, a pleasant feeling or positive sensation experienced in your body and your mind. A sense of generosity, appreciation, and gladness toward the self and the self you have created over a lifetime.

Write about yourself in the third person here, using your own name. The goal here is to create phrases using positive, kind words and messages that fill you with a sense of being cared for, safe, loved, appreciated, and known for who you truly are:

"_____, *you are*

_____."

"_____, *you are*

"

Look at the words you've written and take them in. **How does it feel to be kind and open and accepting of yourself? Do you feel calmer, more peaceful? Do you feel a greater sense of love and care toward yourself?**

What do you notice in your body as you take in your truth? You might feel lighter, more present, open, or safe.

Creating Phrases of Comfort: Messages of Self-Care and Loving-Kindness

Now, I invite you to check in with your benefactors and your older, wiser self once again and see what messages of care they might have to offer you, too.

Instructions

Imagine that your benefactors and your older wiser self are sitting with you, surrounding you, and supporting you. **Now, what are the words you most want to hear whispered in your ear by those who wish the very best for you?**

_____

_____

_____

_____

_____

_____

_____

_____

Perhaps you long to hear words such as, "I will protect you." Or, "I will do everything to keep you safe." Or, "I value and respect you." Or, "You are loved just as you are." Or, "Be kind to yourself." Or, "Trust and believe in yourself."

Write down whatever comes to mind, whatever words you feel would be comforting and reassuring to hear from your older, wiser self, or your benefactors.

_____

_____

_____

_____

_____

What words would help you to feel safe, known, and loved?

_____

_____

_____

_____

_____

_____

Allow yourself to feel the wisdom that these inner beings can provide for you, as they let you know what you need to hear. Now we're going to use these messages to create new meditative phrases of comfort.

Please take these phrases of comfort that you long to hear whispered in your ear and now rewrite them as loving-kindness wishes that you bestow on yourself.

Examples

- "May I know I am safe and protected."

- "May I be valued and loved."

- "May I be kind to myself."

- "May I know that I am enough, just as I am."

- "May I feel safe, genuine connection in my relationships."

- "May I trust and believe in myself."

- "May I feel healthy and vibrant."

What are the loving-kindness wishes you will take with you?

_____

_____

_____

_____

Write these phrases of comfort—your messages of self-care and loving-kindness—on Post-it notes to keep in various places as you go about your day. Perhaps in your sock drawer, or on your desk, or on the back of your smartphone. (Feel free to choose among the different Post-it notes you've created and put some in noticeable places some days, and some on other days, depending on what speaks most to you.)

(This meditation was inspired by the meditation "Finding Loving-Kindness Phrases" by Kristin Neff and Chris Germer 2018).

Self-Care Activity: Couple a Positive Emotion with Physical Movement

Coupling a positive emotion with physical movement can help make positive thoughts more habitual and enhance the process of neural re-narrating.

Look back at the positive wishes you've just written. Allow any positive feelings these phrases bring up in you to arise.

Now let's accompany this sense of growing emotional comfort with a comforting physical movement.

It can help if your movement involves crossing your arms over the midline of the body.

For instance, you might circle the fingers of your right hand in the palm of your left hand as you repeat your phrases of comfort to yourself. Then switch and circle the fingers of your left hand in the palm of your right hand.

Or perhaps cross your arms in front of you, putting your right hand on your left upper arm and your left hand on your right upper arm. Now smooth each hand down over the opposite arm in a slow, soothing movement, the way you might run your hands down the arms of a child to calm them.

Repeat and continue this movement as you continue to repeat your phrases of comfort—messages of self-care and loving-kindness—to yourself.

Feel It, Draw It

Choose one thing you've written in this journal that feels most healing and comforting—a positive *truth* about your younger self, words whispered in your ear from a benefactor, or the phrases of comfort you created for yourself. Write it down again here:

Circle that statement over and over again, letting your pencil go around and around. Think of your benefactors, your older, wiser self, circling and comforting you now.

Take a few moments to make this feeling more than words, breathe it in to every cell, know it on every level of your being, and embody it.

Take two minutes to make a simple drawing, sketch, or doodle that signifies this truth about who you really are and symbolizes these key words you need to hear right now: an image to remind yourself of this feeling. You might think of this as your personal emblem or logo.

Consider taking a picture or photocopy of this personal logo or symbol and placing it where you can see it, especially in those locations where you might be more likely to feel stressed or overwhelmed: your desk, computer screen, bathroom mirror, car visor, or the front of your refrigerator.

Visualize Feeling Different and Better

This visualization activity is adapted from *The Adverse Childhood Experiences Recovery Workbook: Heal the Hidden Wounds from Childhood Affecting Your Adult Mental and Physical Health* by Glenn R. Schiraldi.

When you go to bed tonight, imagine that you wake up tomorrow feeling a sense of lightness, well-being, in a pleasant way. What would that feel like?

_____

_____

_____

_____

Imagine opening your eyes and having the sense that something is different, easier, more pleasant, about your life. Where would you feel that in your body?

_____

_____

_____

_____

Part 7: Call to Action

Hold the hand of the child that lives in your soul.
For this child, nothing is impossible.
—Paulo Coelho

Looking back at your life, you may notice that your most difficult experiences have led you to pursue and achieve new and meaningful layers of healing. Every adversity you face in your life gives you an opportunity to show up in new ways for yourself, stand up for what you need, and take care of yourself in a new way.

Take a moment and give yourself credit for all the internal resources that brought you to this moment, and how your fortitude and desire to be on your own side and flourish helped you to survive challenges in your childhood, as well as the current stressors you face in your everyday adult life. Consider how the stressors in your life, past and present, brought you here to do this work and learn new tools to help you through your darkest moments so that you can ride the waves of life with less suffering.

Every adversity gives you an opportunity to show up
in new ways for yourself, stand up for what you need,
and take care of yourself in a new way.

I believe that there comes a magical moment in every flourisher's healing journey when you realize that you are not broken by events or adversities you've faced over your lifetime; you never were. In fact, you have always held deep within you the resources for flourishing and to love and care for yourself. Indeed, those resources led you right here right now.

In Life's Most Difficult Moments

Salutogenesis: The concept that those who've experienced trauma find flourishing by creating a new narrative, one which arises from within them. This new narrative offers a means of understanding your life in a more meaningful way and allows you to draw upon interior resources to cope with current stressors in your life.

One of the goals of this journal has been to help your brain to create new pathways that improve your mental and physical health by bringing down your stress response. This will help you feel calmer and more centered as you respond to the world around you, especially in difficult or overwhelming situations. We all face situations in our lives that require clear thinking and decision-making, and one of the benefits of this work can be to gain greater clarity in such situations. It is difficult to re-center and stay calm when we are facing immediate and present crises.

Now, we will draw together and integrate all of the work you've done in a way that I hope will lead to better clarity when you are in the midst of crises or overwhelming moments in your life.

* It is important to note here that harmful stressors such as social injustice, racism, discrimination, poverty, abuse, and sexism cannot be adequately addressed merely by changing how one responds to difficult interactions. These must be addressed at a more comprehensive level beyond this book.

Self-Care Activity: My Inner Circle of Self

Imagine that you are sitting at a round table that is encircled in white light.

Seated all around you in chronological order of age are your various selves at different stages and phases of your life. Your past selves might include your five-year-old self, your teenager self, your young adult self, the you of ten years ago, and the you of just five years ago.

Now, going at your own pace, invite your future selves to the table: yourself of a year or two from now, your wiser self of ten years from now, and so on.

Begin to go around the circle of these past and future selves and ask each of them to offer you a message as the light shines down around you all.

Imagine a circle of light surrounds each one of them, their face, and their being, as they offer you a message.

Listen carefully to what each one has to say, and as they speak, take in their words, as if their words are traveling across a ribbon of white light that ties them to you and fills your heart.

For instance, perhaps the five-year-old might say, "Keep me safe." And you might tell her, "I will keep you safe."

Perhaps the teenager might say, "I never thought we'd do so many things in our life or come so far." Or, "Those were such difficult years, and I was sometimes afraid, but look at all that you've done since in your life. We're okay."

Who is around the table with you?

_____

_____

_____

_____

What are they saying?

_____

_____

_____

_____

_____

_____

_____

_____

_____

As they offer their messages, you might respond to these messages of love from your heart.

You might find yourself responding to your teenage self with, "We have come so far, and I wish I could have let you know back then that we would be okay one day."

Perhaps your younger self from the middle years of your life might say, "Wow, look at how we got through all of that and survived." You might respond, "We have courage, don't we? We've been through so much and are coming to a place of peace, aren't we?"

Your older, wiser self might say something like, "You are safe, I will keep you safe. You are beautiful, you are loved, you are courageous."

You might say something in return like, "Thank you for guiding me, for helping me to find healing and to learn how to thrive along the way."

Respond to each part from the heart. What do you want to say in response to your younger or older self?

_____

_____

_____

_____

_____

_____

_____

_____

_____

Take all of these messages in, as all the ribbons of light extending from each self you have been and will be in your life surround you as white vibrating beams of light.

Now let these ribbons of white love and healing messages, and all the selves in your circle, come toward you and meld into your heart.

As they do, place both hands over your heart and feel this love and sense of goodness.

Building Your Inner Flourishing Toolkit

One thing we have learned about trauma is the way in which it leads us to struggle with interpretations and perceptions in ways that can cause us to overreact or underreact, especially when we are caught in difficult interactions in relationships with partners, family, children, and coworkers.

The following neural re-narrating exercise can help you respond differently in these situations. Think about a difficult relationship, challenging interaction, or situation that brings up heightened "sticky" emotions, making it hard for you to calm or soothe yourself. Now ask yourself the following four questions:

1. **Is this a situation you *want*?** For instance, a partner not acknowledging your needs or feelings; a teenager being surly; a coworker unfairly blaming you. Ask yourself, "Do I want X behavior/response/dynamic or to be treated in Y way?" Most likely your answer to this question is NO. Take a moment to acknowledge your feelings. (This might include frustration, hurt, resentment, or feeling you're being treated unfairly.)

2. **Do you *deserve* to have this situation be different?** For example, be with a partner who can support you and hear your feelings, dialogue with a teenager who responds to you with respect, have a coworker who values your work, have a parent who believes in you. Most likely your answer to this question is YES.

   Take a moment to acknowledge how it feels to want something you are not receiving. What emotions come up for you? (This might include disappointment, frustration, grief):

3. **Is this person in my life speaking kindly, allowing me to express my feelings, valuing me, showing me respect?** Your answer to this question might be NO.

   Again, take a moment to write about how this feels for you:

   _____

   _____

   _____

   _____

   _____

   _____

   _____

   _____

4. **Finally, ask yourself, "How can I take care of *myself* and manage these emotions that I am having right now?"** Now, set out to soothe your own nervous system. It's okay if your feelings (loss, anger) are incongruent to the feelings you are trying to help yourself feel now (centered, calm, soothed).

Calm Your Nervous System

Use any combination of the exercises you've learned in this journal, whatever might resonate for you, to help you take care of yourself, and to regulate yourself. Consider other resources: journal a bit more about your feelings, exercise, dance, sing, hum.

When you've taken time to calm your nervous system, you can better observe what is happening rather than stay enmeshed in these dynamics, take part in them, or even make what's happening worse.

Observe the Dynamic

By doing this work, you will be better able to observe these dynamics as you regulate your own emotions rather than be drawn into them or contribute to them. You can more clearly observe what is happening and what isn't happening. This simple step of observing will give you a lot of clarity and prevent you from feeling confused or getting caught in rumination, so that you can take care of you.

Over time, you will be able to self-regulate when overwhelming events occur, especially in interpersonal relationships, and gain clarity about what is best for you in terms of any decisions or actions you may want to take. These decisions could be to suggest couples or family counseling, to apologize if you overreacted to your teenager and set new limits, or to start searching for a new job.

The above technique was taught to me by Marla Sanzone, PhD.

Self-Care Activity: Your Calming Toolkit

Gently close your eyes. Imagine the goodness within your younger self—that core *truth* of who you really are—as a warm, gold, or silver thread that extends forward from childhood throughout the entire timeline of your life, all the way to right here and right now.

Repeat your core words that reflect the truth of your younger self's goodness.

Now, take a moment to stand up and place both hands over your heart.

Keep one hand over your heart and the other over your belly.

Move your hand up from your belly and gently place the tip of your forefinger against your lips. This helps to stimulate the calming effect of the nervous system.

Keeping your eyes closed, look up toward the top of your head.

Slightly stagger your feet and begin to gently rock.

Taking in this good feeling, allow this gold-silver thread to extend from the past into here and now, like a warm light flowing into your heart. Feel the warmth of that light.

Now bring in whatever phrase of comfort or message of love, comfort, self-care, or loving-kindness phrase that you've created for yourself and resonates most with you.

Drink in this warm light, this feeling, this truth about YOU, and this message of safety that you most need to hear.

Imagine this light entering your heart, warming and illuminating it. Let it expand out of your heart into your entire chest and throughout your body, your torso, your arms and legs, and up into the top of your head.

Feel it expand and shine out from the top of your head and down through the soles of your feet, and from the front and back of your heart, so that this light extends into a globe circling around you.

Bask in this feeling of calm and safety that you have created for yourself.

Flourishing Through Neural Re-Narrating—Your Truth

Now, let's create a space to return to the next time you feel overwhelmed with big feelings, or feel old, familiar thought cycles come up that have you caught in ruminating, or if you're lashing out at yourself for something you feel you could or should have done differently.

First, call in your resources, your benefactors.

In the space below, write your core truths about your essential goodness and worthiness and the positive attributes of your inner child. You may want to return to previous pages of this journal for inspiration.

Write the phrases of comfort that have most resonated with you.

Practice saying these different phrases and going within and seeing which ones make you feel most at peace with yourself and in harmony with the world around you.

Please pick one positive inner truth and one phrase of comfort that most resonate for you. Now, using your smartphone or other recording device, record yourself speaking your truth and your meditative phrases of comfort to yourself. Throughout the day, play the recording of you soothing and comforting yourself whenever you are feeling overwhelmed.

Be sure to also take in the messages on the Post-it notes you have put in places where you will see them frequently, such as your desktop or your bathroom mirror. You might even make one your background on your smartphone or take a photo of all of your Post-it notes and make this the wallpaper on your personal computer.

Throughout the day, return to your audio and written messages to remind yourself of the most healing moments that resonated for you while on this journey.

As you do, you might bring in your benefactors and hear them offer these messages to you, whispered in your ear.

The invitation here is to invite this truth about who you are and your phrases of comfort into the moments in your present life when you feel overwhelmed, and to do so with a sense of compassion, joy, and gratitude for who you are.

Draw upon your truth. Revel in it. It is yours.

Try as best you can to recall and repeat your truth and your phrases of comfort, especially when you're under stress or feeling overwhelmed, feeling angry with those around you, or if you find yourself caught up in ruminating thought cycles.

Validating these positive aspects of how you adapted in the face of past adversity while letting go of the less-helpful ways in which you may have coped—such as harmful self-narratives that no longer serve you—offers you deep, new internal resources for healing, thriving, and flourishing, even in the face of adversity.

 Conclusion

Now, I'd like you to reflect on your entire experience in writing your story of YOU. You've hopefully had many moments in this journal in which you've felt a sense of gladness about who you are, your courage, goodness, and fortitude. And I hope you've also experienced a glimmer of feeling safe and at home within yourself, right now, and been able to embody those feelings.

In part 1 of this book, you contemplated your own story of childhood adversity and wrote down a few words to capture whatever came immediately to mind. **Now that you are nearing the end of this book and seeing the truth of who you are and your worthiness and courage in the face of difficult challenges across your life, what words come to mind now to sum up your own story?** (These might be words like, "I understand and honor my own story" or, "I always lead with love.") There are no right words. Just choose the first few words that come to mind.

Now after writing about your journey and leaning more deeply into the goodness of who you really are, if you were to give your own story a movie or book title, what would that be? Be creative. Don't overthink it! It might be similar to "A Story of Love and Courage" or "How I Learned to Love Myself" or "The One Who Learned to Love and Be Loved." Make this your own!

Continuing and Deepening Your Healing Journey

I hope that through this journal you have come to understand the way in which adversity in childhood and other life stressors can impact your mental and physical health. I hope you've begun to make the crucial mental shift from responding to stress with old, entrenched thought patterns and habits that may no longer serve you to feeling confident about the new approaches and strategies you learned while completing this journal. These strategies will help you to respond to overwhelming feelings and situations in your life in less reactive and healthier ways, and with self-love.

And I hope you've come to see the benefits of writing-to-heal and neural re-narrating in your healing journey. Over time, when you engage in these practices with a sense of self-compassion, you can begin to change your mood, your health, your relationships, and your life. I also hope you see the power of making a commitment to yourself, out of loyalty to yourself, to continue on this healing journey after this journal is completed.

Healing is about far more than fixing what we feel we are doing wrong. It is about building on and creating a strong identification with all that is good and worthy within you and has always been within you. Healing happens within those moments in which we create a sense of interior safety and well-being.

As you begin to focus more on what gives you a deeper sense of release, safety, calm, and rest your attention there, over time, you'll increase your ability to flourish even in difficult moments.

Finally, as you continue on your healing journey, remember it's heroic to heal your own wounds. By doing so, you help to model and show others how to do the same.

Please—if you find that you are feeling overwhelmed as you complete this journal or need more support than that which a journaling experience can provide, please reach out to a therapist or counselor.

 Continuing Your Healing Journey

Commit to Doing Something Small Every Day

Every day, please take five minutes and practice one of the self-care, self-talk, breath, or mindfulness exercises learned. Usually we know and recognize what is most helpful to us on our pathway to healing in our effort to live a better and more easeful and joyful life. Different practices will be very powerful for different people. Commit to those that resonate for you.

Retake the Joy Quotient Questionnaire

In one week, after practicing for at least five minutes a day, please retake the final questionnaire, the Joy Quotient questionnaire, and see if you are experiencing more moments of joy and contentment. Compare your answers after one week to your answers prior to completing this journal and see if anything has changed for you. Even very small changes can add up over time.

Return to Your Journal—or Start Another!

Have fun with the journal you have created that captures the story of you. Make it your own. You might tie it together with ribbons, add in more photos or drawings—you can make it as much of an art project as you want it to be! After this journal is full, you might begin another healing journal and return to your favorite prompts and exercises or write your own! You can find bonus materials at the website for this book, http://www.newharbinger.com/54155. There you can download bonus prompts and audio versions of some meditations.

    Thank you for taking the time to complete your journal and rewrite your story. I hope you feel a deeper sense of self-compassion and have learned a series of new life-enhancing practices that will help you to flourish as you continue on your healing path!

Additional Resources

Powerful Mindfulness Techniques for Grounding and Centering

Mindfulness training can help individuals find a deep source of relief from overidentifying with emotions, memories, or thoughts.

Dan Siegel, MD, and the Wheel of Awareness

One such powerful meditation is the Wheel of Awareness created by Dan Siegel, MD. The Wheel of Awareness is an excellent tool to help you understand and practice mindful awareness and is unusual in that it includes three types of mindfulness: focused attention, open awareness, and kind intention, which can enhance neurobiological resilience (Villamil et al. 2019). For more on how to practice this meditation, see www.drdansiegel.com/wheel-of-awareness.

Tara Brach, PhD, and RAIN

Tara Brach, PhD, offers a range of meditation practices, including a practice called RAIN that can guide you in bringing mindfulness and compassion to difficult emotions. Visit www.tarabrach.com for more.

Kristen Neff, PhD, and Self-Compassion

Kristen Neff, PhD, provides an array of self-compassion meditations that can help you offer the same kindness and support to yourself that you would offer a good friend. Visit **www.self-compassion.org** for more.

Finding a Mental Health Practitioner

If you are seeking a mental health care practitioner in your area, visit **https://www .psychologytoday.com/us/therapists**.

If you or anyone you know is in crisis, please contact the National Suicide Prevention Lifeline at 988.

Acknowledgments

I've spent my writing career trying to help those who are suffering by offering hope on the page. This book is the culmination of years of listening to thousands of individuals' stories and witnessing how a curious sort of healing begins to occur when we narrate—and listen to—our own stories.

Over the years, I've seen that when we create a meaningful narrative around what happened to us, we're better able to understand our own story and see links between our past and present life experiences. We're able to appreciate our perseverance, courage, and worthiness, often for the first time. Witnessing YOUR courageous journeys toward healing in my workshops and courses has moved me to create this workbook. Thank you for showing me the way and inspiring me.

This book would not exist without many great teachers and neuroscientists whose work has touched me, many of whom are cited on the resources page of this book.

Every writer needs a visionary editor. I'm grateful for Tesilya Hanauer, who first saw the potential for this book (and patiently waited for it while I finished another); it is an absolute joy to work with you. Every writer needs a champion; in this I'm blessed to have my lifelong agent, Elizabeth Kaplan. Thank you, too, to Madison Davis for helping to shape this book, and Amber Williams for your copyediting.

Most importantly, to my husband, son, daughter, and friends (you know who you are because we've shared our stories), the gift of being lucky enough to know and love you and share life's inevitable woes and joys makes this life so much better than I ever could have imagined.

References

Angelou, M. 2009. *Letter to My Daughter*. New York: Random House.

Bethell, C., J. Jones, N. Gombojav, J. Linkenbach, and R. Sage. 2019. "Positive Childhood Experiences and Adult Mental and Relationship Health in a Statewide Sample." *JAMA Pediatrics* 173(11): e193007.

Brown, E. M., K. Carlisle, M. Burgess, J. Clark, and A. Hutcheon. 2022. "Adverse and Positive Childhood Experiences of Clinical Mental Health Counselors as Predictors of Compassion Satisfaction, Burnout, and Secondary Traumatic Stress." *The Professional Counselor* 12(1): 49–64.

California Surgeon General's Clinical Advisory Committee. 2020. "Adverse Childhood Experiences Questionnaire for Adults." *ACEs Aware*, May 5. https://www.aces aware.org/wp-content/uploads/2022/07/ACE-Questionnaire-for-Adults-Identified -English-rev.7.26.22.pdf.

Centers for Disease Control and Prevention (CDC). n.d. "Violence Prevention: Adverse Childhood Experiences." https://www.cdc.gov/violenceprevention/aces.

Clark, C. S., and A. E.-M. Aboueissa. 2021. "Nursing Students' Adverse Childhood Experience Scores: A National Survey." *International Journal of Nursing Education Scholarship* 18(1): 20210013.

Coelho, P. 2014. "Hold the hand of the child within you." Facebook, September 3. https://www.facebook.com/paulocoelho/photos/a.241365541210/101526338072 16211/?type=3.

Cohen, S., D. Janicki-Deverts, W. J. Doyle, G. E. Miller, E. Frank, B. S. Rabin, and R. B. Turner. 2012. "Chronic Stress, Glucocorticoid Receptor Resistance, Inflammation, and Disease Risk." *Proceedings of the National Academy of Sciences* 109(16): 5995–5999.

Desch, J., F. Mansuri, D. Tran, S. W. Schwartz, and C. Bakour. 2023. "The Association Between Adverse Childhood Experiences and Depression Trajectories in the ADD Health Study." *Child Abuse and Neglect* 137: 106034.

Dube, S. R., D. Fairweather, W. S. Pearson, V. J. Felitti, R. F. Anda, and J. B. Croft. 2009. "Cumulative Childhood Stress and Autoimmune Diseases in Adults." *Psychosomatic Medicine* 71(2): 243–250.

Glass, O., M. Dreusicke, J. Evans, E. Bechard, and R. Q. Wolever. 2019. "Expressive Writing to Improve Resilience to Trauma: A Clinical Feasibility Trial." *Complementary Therapies in Clinical Practice* 34: 240–246.

Glenn, M. 2018. "The Vagus Nerve and Your Health." *Ryzio*, August 8. https://ryzio.com /self-help/vagus-nerve-your-health.

Hurston, Z. N. 1942. *Dust Tracks on a Road: An Autobiography by Zora Neale Hurston*. Philadelphia: J. B. Lippincott Company.

Jackson Nakazawa, D. 2013. *The Last Best Cure: My Quest to Awaken the Healing Parts of My Brain and Get Back My Body, My Joy, and My Life*. New York: Hudson Street Press.

Jahren, H. 2017. *Lab Girl*. New York: Vintage.

Jones, P. A. 2019. "Hiraeth." *Haggard Hawks* (blog), September 11. https://www.haggard hawks.com/post/hiraeth.

Lin, I. M., L. Y. Tai, and S. Y. Fan. 2014. "Breathing at a Rate of 5.5 Breaths Per Minute with Equal Inhalation-to-Exhalation Ratio Increases Heart Rate Variability." *International Journal of Psychophysiology* 91(3): 206–211.

MacKenett, K. 2018. "Earthquakes." Facebook, August 21. https://www.facebook.com/ KatherineMacKenettWriter/posts/pfbid027rw9C69QE9rrJRbrnfieCtEgc2R8P-bAMXLWrgDwnDHDfni33aMktP4RHt9YHcdW7l.

Neff, K., and C. Germer. 2018. *The Mindful Self-Compassion Workbook: A Proven Way to Accept Yourself, Build Inner Strength, and Thrive*. New York: Guilford.

Pennebaker, J. W., J. K. Kiecolt-Glaser, and R. Glaser. 1988. "Disclosure of Traumas and Immune Function: Health Implications for Psychotherapy." *Journal of Consulting and Clinical Psychology* 56(2): 239–245.

Schiraldi, G. R. 2021. *The Adverse Childhood Experiences Recovery Workbook: Heal the Hidden Wounds from Childhood Affecting Your Adult Mental and Physical Health*. Oakland, CA: New Harbinger.

Siegel, D. J. 2014. *Brainstorm: The Power and Purpose of the Teenage Brain*. New York: TarcherPerigee.

Tian, T., J. Li, G. Zhang, J. Wang, D. Liu, C. Wan, J. Fang, et al. 2021. "Default Mode Network Alterations Induced by Childhood Trauma Correlate with Emotional Function and SLCA4 Expression." *Frontiers in Psychiatry* 12: 760411.

Tieicher, M. H., and J. A. Samson. 2016. "Annual Research Review: Enduring Neurobiological Effects of Childhood Abuse and Neglect." *Journal of Child Psychology and Psychiatry* 57(3): 241–266.

Torre, J. B., and M. D. Lieberman. 2018. "Putting Feelings into Words: Affect Labeling as Implicit Emotion Regulation." *Emotion Review* 10(2): 116–124.

Villamil, A., T. Vogel, E. Weisbaum, and D. J. Siegel. 2019. "Cultivating Well-Being Through the Three Pillars of Mind Training: Understanding How Training the Mind Improves Physiological and Psychological Well-Being." *OBM Integrative and Complementary Medicine* 4(1).

Weder, N., H. Zhang, K. Jensen, B. Z. Yang, A. Simen, A. Jackowski, D. Lipschitz, et al. 2014. "Child Abuse, Depression, and Methylation in Genes Involved with Stress, Neural Plasticity, and Brain Circuitry." *Journal of the American Academy of Child and Adolescent Psychiatry* 53(4): 417–424.

Donna Jackson Nakazawa is creator of Your Healing Narrative, the writing-to-heal program that uses the Neural Re-Narrating process she pioneered. She is author of *Girls on the Brink*, and the best-selling *Childhood Disrupted*. She has lectured and taught at major universities and organizations, and is a frequent contributor to national news programs and publications.

Foreword writer **Nedra Glover Tawwab, LCSW**, is author of *Drama Free* and *Set Boundaries, Find Peace*. A licensed therapist and sought-after relationship expert, she has practiced relationship therapy for more than fifteen years. She lives in Charlotte, NC, with her family.

MORE BOOKS from
NEW HARBINGER PUBLICATIONS

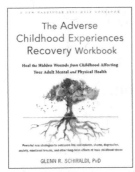

**THE ADVERSE
CHILDHOOD EXPERIENCES
RECOVERY WORKBOOK**

Heal the Hidden Wounds from
Childhood Affecting Your Adult
Mental and Physical Health

978-1684036646 / US $24.95

**SELF-CARE FOR
ADULT CHILDREN
OF EMOTIONALLY
IMMATURE PARENTS**

Honor Your Emotions,
Nurture Your Self, and
Live with Confidence

978-1684039821 / US $18.95

**SIMPLE WAYS TO UNWIND
WITHOUT ALCOHOL**

50 Tips to Drink Less
and Enjoy More

978-1648482342 / US $18.95

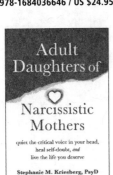

**ADULT DAUGHTERS OF
NARCISSISTIC MOTHERS**

Quiet the Critical Voice
in Your Head, Heal Self-Doubt,
and Live the Life You Deserve

978-1648480096 / US $18.95

**50 WAYS TO REWIRE YOUR
ANXIOUS BRAIN**

Simple Skills to Soothe
Anxiety and Create New
Neural Pathways to Calm

978-1648481789 / US $16.95

**HEAL YOUR PAST TO
MANIFEST YOUR FUTURE**

Trauma-Informed Practices to
Release Emotional Blocks and
Open to Life's Possibilities

978-1648483042 / US $21.95
ⓇREVEAL PRESS
An Imprint of New Harbinger Publications

🌱 **newharbinger**publications

1-800-748-6273 / newharbinger.com

(VISA, MC, AMEX / prices subject to change without notice)

Follow Us 📷 f 𝕏 ▶ ⓟ in ♪ ⓖ

Did you know there are **free tools** you can download for this book?

Free tools are things like **worksheets**, **guided meditation exercises**, and **more** that will help you get the most out of your book.

You can download free tools for this book—whether you bought or borrowed it, in any format, from any source—from the New Harbinger website. All you need is a NewHarbinger.com account. Just use the URL provided in this book to view the free tools that are available for it. Then, click on the "download" button for the free tool you want, and follow the prompts that appear to log in to your NewHarbinger.com account and download the material.

You can also save the free tools for this book to your **Free Tools Library** so you can access them again anytime, just by logging in to your account! Just look for this button on the book's free tools page.

+ Save this to my free tools library

If you need help accessing or downloading free tools, visit **newharbinger.com/faq** or contact us at **customerservice@newharbinger.com**.